The Guthrie Saga

including the
Diary of Andrew J. Guthrie
1877–1883

Author, current photograph.

The Guthrie Saga

*including the
Diary of Andrew J. Guthrie
1877–1883*

BY

ANDREW GUTHRIE MACDOUGALL

The Pentland Press Limited
Edinburgh · Cambridge · Durham · USA

First published in 1998 by
The Pentland Press Ltd.
1 Hutton Close
South Church
Bishop Auckland
Durham

British Library Cataloguing in Publication Data.
A catalogue record for this book is available
from the British Library.

ISBN 1 85821 568 4

Typeset by George Wishart & Associates, Whitley Bay.
Printed and bound by Bookcraft Ltd., Bath.

To the Department of Veteran Affairs
my wife and I will be eternally grateful

THE LAND I'M LEAVING BEHIND

My barque leaves the harbour tomorrow
Across the wide ocean to go
But Kitty my burden of sorrow
Is more that I'd wish you to know
There's a dreary dark cloud hanging o'er me
And a mighty big load on my mind
When I think on the prospect before me
And the country I'm leaving behind

Chorus Farewell to the green fields of Erin
       Farewell to the hearts true and kind
       But where ere I may be, I will still think of thee

And the country I'm leaving behind
Now Kitty 'give over' your crying
And don't be uneasy for me
It's my fortune I'd be after trying
In the sunny land over the sea
But each moment that passes shall find thee
Reigning supreme in my mind
But the image of Kitty shall bind me
To the country I'm leaving behind

Though the land be abounding with treasure
And fair maid of every degree
Though my eyes may behold them with pleasure
My heart will be longing for thee
Though stormy clouds gather above me
And friendship prove stale or unkind
I well know there is one heart that loves me
In the country I'm leaving behind

CONTENTS

ILLUSTRATIONS

PREFACE

This book spans four wars; the Zulu War and the North West Frontier of India; then a mention of the 1914–18 war and finally the 1939–45 war with Germany and Japan.

My grandfather, Andrew J. Guthrie last known address, 60 Mansion street, Possilpark, Glasgow, enlisted in the 2nd Battalion, Scottish rifles in 1877 and kept a diary in perfect copperplate writing until his discharge in 1883. My niece Doris Henderson has put his diary into print.

My uncle, Andrew Guthrie was in the 1914–18 war and died of wounds in October 1918, two months before I was born.

I, Andrew Guthrie Macdougall, served in the 1939–45 war from March 1940 until July 1941 in England, thence overseas to Singapore where I was captured by Japs on 17th March 1942. I worked on the Burma Thailand Railway from October 1942 to 12th December 1944, before being transferred to Thailand. I was released on 17th August 1945 from camp Nakhon Nie in Thailand.

My mother, Rebecca Guthrie, married my father,

My grandfather Andrew J. Guthrie, trainer Kent FC football club, far left. His son (my uncle) Andrew Guthrie to the right of the soccer ball, died in the 1914–18 war aged 21. Photograph pre 1914.

Donald Forbes Macdougall, at the start of the 1914–18 war. He was the son of Alexander Macdougall who came from Balnald Farm, Fortingall and who was married to Isabella Forbes, age 20, of 24 Pitt Street, the daughter of Alexander Forbes, coach-hirer, on the 12th February 1869, at 24 Pitt Street, after banns were called according to the forms of the Church of Scotland.

My father at the time of his marriage was a fully qualified journeyman tailor, but within a year or two he was struck down healthwise by one of the most horrible diseases which can affect humanity namely locomotor ataxia, a progressive disease of the nervous system which affects the lower part of the spinal cord. He went blind first, then lost the mobility of his legs and was bed ridden until his death in 1937. My mother faithfully attended to him for twenty years. I was at his bedside when our doctor arrived and we knew it was the end. The doctor measured out a spoon containing morphine and at last he was at peace within minutes.

We had moved from 2 Leyden Street, Maryhill, to 580 Balmore Road, Lambhill where there were wide open spaces. We had quite a distance to travel to school at North Kelvinside Senior Secondary School, and we always took a short cut across Ruchill Golf Course.

My sister Betty went to the local school where she met Mary Thom and they are still great friends after more than sixty years. Best of all, Mary had a brother, Jim, who came up to see me and from then on I was never away from the stables, which was an old established firm. I won't go into too much of what we did, but one evening Jim had this horse out for a run and he would have it that I got on the horse behind him. Off we went, on a track at the back of the police station. The going at that time was pretty rough, mostly ashes. We turned to go back and Jim increased the tempo; on we flew till we hit a rough track; the horse went down, and Jim and I flew over its head. We were lucky, Jim's dad came on the scene and was he mad. He examined the horse and did he give Jim what for. 'You have knocked out the horse's stifle', at least that is what I thought he said. However the horse came good and both Jim and I heaved a sigh of relief. I was 12 years old at the time.

Two years later at the age of 14 I started work, as a messenger boy, with J & A McFarlane, 40 Springbank Street, Maryhill (the premises are now demolished) and at 19 was in charge of one of the departments. I took up badminton as a sport in St Matthews Church in Balmore Road near the Mecca Cinema. We played quite a few matches in competition with other clubs. I had a great partner there, Miss Cathie Bain, who was the sister of William Bain, a classmate of mine in North Kelvinside School. One of the girls where I worked was a keen badminton player and I invited her up to our club as a guest, her name Betty Campbell. I met her later in dramatic circumstances.

PART 1

Andrew J. Guthrie's Story

THE GEIKA WAR

Life of one of Cardwells Short Service Men at home and abroad from 4th April 1877 to 20th June 1883 A.J. Guthrie 2nd Battalion S. Rifles

1877 April 4. On this day I found myself in Maryborough, Queen's County, Ireland. Rather out of place certainly, and being out of pocket also, I thought the best thing to put in it was the Queen's Shilling. So I made the best of my way to the militia staff barracks I seen the Sergeant Major and asked if they were recruiting for the line. I was shown into the orderly room and there being a standard there, I was measured. I was tall enough (and 2 1/2 inches to spare) for the line. They were recruiting for the infantry only, during the time I was getting measured the doctor came in and I was taken into another room and examined and passed fit for to make a target to be shot at. I then got my enlisting shilling and 1/6d, my days pay, and was told to come the following morning to be sworn in.

1877 April 5. I made my appearance at the barracks

in due time and was taken to Dr Hamilton's, a Justice of Peace where I was duly sworn to Her Majesty, Heirs and Successors for the term of 6 years in the army, 6 years in the reserve and 12 months longer if my services were required.

[Pages missing]

1877 Wrong. I was soon passed by my comrades as a Don at drinking, quarelling and rather too well aquainted with the character that resorted the bars of The Fountain Royal Arms, Aldershot Arms, etc. enough of that, I was young and foolish, and among strangers, nothing to occupy my mind except beer, tobacco and –//–.

1877 October 7th. The 100th Regiment paraded at 4 a.m. to proceed to Portsmouth where they were to embark for the East India's. I and several others volunteered to go with them, but we would not be allowed, all being under 20 years of age.

1877 October 18th. I was appointed Lance Corpl., the first step to a court martial, as it eventually proved to be in my case.

1877 October 20th. The 67th Brigade Depots 100th and 109th paraded at 6.45 a.m. to proceed to Portsmouth to do duty in Clarence barracks where we arrived in due time and took over the barracks and were confined to barracks for that evening.

1877 October 21st. Being on no duty that afternoon I went to see the town. I thought a great deal of the fortifications but more of the Bulls Head just outside the gate where I was a regular attender. Portsmouth is the best place I ever soldiered in. That good in fact that I was glad to leave it for Gosport.

1877 December 18th. 18 Men, 1 Lance Corpl., and 2 Sergts. left Portsmouth for Gosport Forts to get them ready for the Regiment which was expected home from India on the 27th. We were in Fort Roner headquarters were for Fort Grange. The rooms were very small and all underground and very dark.

1877 December 27th. The regiment marched up to the forts at 4 p.m. having disembarked from aboard the Crocodile Indian troopship. For the next few days there was a great deal of drunkeness.

1878 January 2nd. About 5.30 pm I was standing at the fire in my room the Corporal Sergeant of my Company (being acting Sergeant Major of the Fort) was reading orders to the orderly sergeants. I was paying no attention to the reading until I heard him mention the 90th Light Infantry and as we lay in the next lines to them in Aldershott, I listened to hear what was in the orders concerning them. I found they were under orders for the Cape of Good Hope to assist in quelling some disturbance there and they wanted volunteers to make up the Regiment to war strength. Here was a chance to leave the girls of Portsmouth and not to be thrown away. The 90th L.I. was one of the smartest regiments stood Aldershott. So as soon as the orderly sergeants were done, I told the orderly sergeant to put my name down as a volunteer for the 90th. There was 21 of our department volunteered.

1878 January 3rd. We paraded at the orderly room, passed the Commanding Officer and passed the doctor as fit for active service.

1878 January 4th. My comrade came out of hospital and when he heard I had volunteered he went and put his name down at once.

1878 January 7th. We paraded at Fort Grange and were marched over to Anglesea Barracks Portsmouth. We paraded on the square with drafts from 19th, 107th, 55th all for the 90th. We marched to the railway station at 2 pm. We arrived in Aldershott. We marched up to the north camp and was handed over to the Sergeant Major who told us off to our respective companies. My comrade and I were sent to 'C' Company then we could go where we liked until tattoo, of course I went to visit one of my old friends in the town of Aldershott and got you may be certain it was not sober.

1878 January 8th. We were served out with a complete set of equipment. Long bayonet and black helmet, the 90th being the first regiment that got either, men were sent to instruct us in folding coats and packing valises as nearly every regiment has a different way on putting them together.

1878 January 9th. Paraded in marching order for Generals inspection. He said a few words in praise of the regiment as to their good conduct and discipline while under his command. He hoped they would gain a great name where they were going. Then 3 cheers were given for General Anderson and the Parade dismissed.

1878 January 10th. At 5 am the companies CD&E fell in and marched to Farnborough station under command of R.M. Rogers V.C. Major. They left by rail for Southampton where they embarked on board the SS *Danube* for Natal colony.

1878 January 11th. My company, being over 100 strong. I and two more were left behind to go with Headquarters and were attached to "F" Company. So we fell in at 4.30 and marched to the station. The bands of the 4th, 2/25th, 49th and 3/60 played us out to the station then they formed up and as the train was leaving the 4 bands played Auld Lang Syne, we were not long in getting to Southampton. The train ran into the sheds alongside the quay. We were soon told off to messes, 12 men to each. We went on board the S.S. *Nobian*. Shortly afterwards we had breakfast. The rest of the time was employed in drawing plates, dishes, cans and pint tins, blankets and hammocks and at 4pm sailed out of harbour. The men seemed in good spirits, the quay was crowded with civilians cheering and waving handkerchiefs. We then anchored off Ketley Hospital until next morning waiting for the mails.

1878 January 12th. At 5am weighed anchor and stood out to sea passed The Needles and off down the channel.

1878 January 17th. Dropped anchor off Madeira before daybreak and as the morning dawned we could see a large headland off the ships bows and as the morning advanced we could see the outline of large rocks till at length we could see they were cottages whitewashed in the distance. It seemed to be a nice place nicely laid out. Though the streets seemed rather steep. We took on 17 head of cattle and 200 ton of coal. A lot of natives came out in Bum boats selling oranges, bananas, figs and for tobacco, old clothes, knives and they were splendid divers, one was naked sitting in each boat and when we threw a bit of tobacco or a penny into the water in they went and brought it out. We left at noon.

1878 February 4th. We sighted Lions Romp Cape of Good Hope and a promising appearance it had too, not a bit of grass, not a tree or house to be seen. In 2 1/2 hours after sighting land we entered Table Bay and dropped anchor. The sight which now met our view was indeed beautiful. On our right lay Cape Town in all the beauties of a foreign summer. The town is built at the foot of a very high mountain called Table Mountain it being flat on top, at all times of the year a white cloud hangs over the mountain and to see it rolling over the top you would fancy it was a large waterfall. The side of the mountain is covered with evergreen trees and shrubs, gardens of orange trees, figs and grapes. On the right of the town of Fort Amsterdam built by the Dutch and taken from them by the English in 1838. In front of the town on the sea shore is Cape Castle and on the left is the road leading to Wineberg. On our left lay Robin's Island, the convict station for South Africa.

1878 February 5th. At 7 am we steamed into harbour and lay alongside the S.S. *Dublin Castle* with KB5BR on board. We then disembarked 'H' company, all the sick, court-martial prisoners, bands and married women which we had to leave behind. We inquired if the R.A. was going to land there but they did not know.

1878 February 6th. We backed out of harbour and lay to in the bay until 2 pm when we steamed off for East London.

1878 February 7th. Paraded with helmets to get turbans put on to protect us from the sun. About 7 yards of white muslin folded round the helmet and hanging down the back to keep the sun off our necks. There was an order given that no man to leave camp. But for all that there was many amount went out and a picquet had to be sent out to bring them in. They brought in several drunk and carried them to a guardroom and left them.

1878 February 9th. When we awoke in the morning we were lying at anchor and about a mile off lay East London. As far as we could make out there was only a few houses, but what surprised us most was to see a lot of barges coming out to the ship. No one had any idea what they were for. The first 2 ran along side. One for baggage and the other for men. A rope ladder was then lowered over the side and the men began to descend to the barge. But each man had to watch his opportunity to leap as the barge was rocking to and fro on the surf. In time, 150 men were transferred to the hold of the barge and battened down and pulled ashore by ropes. The pier is built at the mouth of a river, and about 300 yds in front, is long line of reefs which cannot be crossed by those barges, even at high tide, without the bottom grating on the reef. They are made specially for this purpose, flat-bottomed and strongly built, but it was horrible to have 150 men huddled like sheep in the stinking hold of a surf boat, as they are called. About 12 noon, all were disembarked. The baggage was then loaded on bullock wagons, the only mode of transport in the country except mules and very few of them. Each wagon is drawn by 14 or 16 bullocks, there in only one shaft to the wagon. At the end of the shaft, there is a chain about 20 yards long. At equal distance apart, sticks are fastened about 4 foot long and about 12 inches in circumference. There are 2 holes at each end about a foot apart, and wooden pegs put in them about a foot long. The bullocks are put after each other in two lines, one each side of the chain. A stick is then lifted and placed on the neck of the first two bullocks, their necks between the two pegs. The pegs are then fastened by a thong of raw hide and their heads are kept together in a similar manner. All the bullocks being sent under their sticks in like manner the harness is complete. Then there is a kafir boy in front, leading the first two. He is, what they call, a forelooper. The driver carried a long whip, made of rawhide, fastened to a long bamboo handle. The wagons being loaded, we fell in and marched about 2 miles to Panmore, where we were to encamp for the night. We were escorted of course by hundreds of blacks, men women and children, almost naked. All the children were naked as the day they were born. The women were not much better off as regards clothing. I noticed several women as we passed by, and their breasts actually hung belong their waists. One woman, rather aged, was standing there with a youngster on her back. It was frightened at the soldiers, and to keep it quiet she put her hand under breast and threw it up to the child without the least difficulty. We had to cross the river on a floating bridge and then marched to the camp. The sun was scorching hot and being in marching order we were nearly fainting by the time we got to camp. There was 4 barrels of water brought for the regiment. Then there was a general rush made for it.

1878 February 10th. The rouse sounded at 5.30am and in a few minutes all hands were up. The first news was that one of the prisoners was dead. A man named Murphy of 'A' Company, having died though the effect of 'Cape Smoke' a kind of liquor, like water in appearance. He was sewed up in a blanket and buried scarcely 10 inches below the surface. We had not time to do more as a special train was in waiting to take us to King Williams Town. Having struck tents and placed them on the trucks with the rest of the baggage, we then got on top of the baggage in the trucks. Two men that were absent came in and the train started. We looked as if we were going to a funeral with our black helmets and white turbans with streamers handing down through. And at the different stations, crowds of blacks were gathered at the platforms to see the soldiers. As for the line I never seen the like since or before, such a zigzag affair no one will ever see unless they travel between East London and King William Town. The turns were so sharp that the men in the last truck could almost shake hands with the engine driver. The stations were Cambridge, Fort Jackson, Blaney Junction and the K. W. Town. We arrived at the station at 12.30. The band of the 1/24 were in waiting to play us into the camping ground at the other side of town. The streets as we marched through, were crowded with men of all nations. At last were arrived at the camping ground, on the side of a hill about 1/2 a mile fron the Cape Horn barracks. Shortly after arriving at the camp ground the tents were pitched, the baggage got up from the station and the cooks began to get ready for dinner. The sun was very strong and the curtains of the tents were rolled up to let the air in, though there was not a breath of wind. The men were lying with their heads out under the curtains, gasping for breath, being nearly stifled from the sun playing on the canvas. By and by we got well used to heat and cold.

1878 February 11th. Unpacking stores, bathing and cleaning arms and equipment. In the afternoon I went to see the town. It is a long straggling place, nothing good looking about it except the barracks and it's not up to much. In rear of the camp is a village of friendly Kafirs and on the right is a Fingoe village, a loyal tribe fighting on the British side, but the Kafirs call them their dogs.

1878 February 12th. Nothing to be done except amuse ourselves the best we could.

1878 February 13th. The order came for fifty men of the Regt. to be struck off duty, to be formed into a mounted infantry corps to act as cavalry. They very soon got men as they allowed them to volunteer. They thought it an easy billet to ride around the country but before they were many days there they wanted to get back to their duty.

1878 February 14th. The Regt. paraded for general inspection by Sir Arthur Cunningham. He spoke of having served with the Regt. at the Crimea and hoped they would distinguish themselves as well in quelling the rebellion in the Cape as the Regt. did before Sebastipol. After some talk about the country the parade was dismissed. At 5pm an order was given for one Coy to proceed to Post Wellington, a detachment about 30 miles away. "F" Coy was detailed for it.

1878 February 15th. At 10am "G" Coy received orders to march at 2pm, to Fort Beaufort, 50 miles, but in the opposite direction from "F" Coy which did not leave until 4pm. as they were to go halfway by train, "G" Coy marched off with 3 wagons for baggage. It was a nice clear day when we marched to the station. At 4 our baggage was taken down to the station and loaded on the trucks. Just as the train was about to start it commenced raining, so the men had to be put into carriages. About one hours ride brought us to Blaney Junction and another brought us to Kie-Road where we got out. It was then dark and still raining. The ground was too wet to pitch tents so we had to remain in the sheds all night without supper. Sentries were posted in front and rear of the shed. "G" Coy fared even worse, they were in an open country and had to march all night, passing a place called Greenriver at 10pm, wet to the skin, with 70 rounds of ammunition round their waists.

1878 February 16th. With 'F' Coy. the rouse sounded at 5.30 a.m. and we turned out of the sheds. We found it was still raining and after standing 3 hours in the rain, waiting for wagons for our baggage, we began our march to Blanes Farm, 9 miles. It rained all day and when we got to the camp the ground was flooded. We could not be any wetter than we were, so we pitched out tents and lay down on the wet

15

ground. The cooks tried to get something to eat ready, but the wood, being wet, it was no easy matter to light a fire. After some time the dinner, or what was called a dinner, was served up and we had to make the best of it. We then lay down in our clothes, the water running round us and we slept as sound as if on a bed of down.

1878 February 17th. Rouse sounded at 5.30 a.m. and all hands were soon employed in striking camp. When it was found that a man of the 88th Connaught Rangers (who was attached to us going up to Komgtha to join his regiment) had found out during the night where the rum was kept. He broke open the barrel and drank that much that he was dead in the morning. We sewed him up in two sacks and buried him at the foot of a tree. The captain of the Coy. read the burial service. After he was buried, we marched on to Fort Wellington, 9 miles. It was still raining and it was 4 p.m. before we got into camp. The roads were so heavy the bullocks could not get along. On arriving there we found 2 Coy 1/24th there, so we had to camp at the foot of the hill until next morning

1878 February 18th. Sun shone out splendid which dried our clothes and cheered us up a little. The 1/24th marched off at 9 a.m. and we pitched our camp on their ground as it was dry.

1878 February 19th. The Companies "G" "A" "B" arrived at Fort Beaufort and received orders to march next day for Water Kloof.

1878 February 20th. Left Beaufort early in the morning. It was raining very heavy. The men had to get drag ropes and pull the wagons up the hills and had to lie down in the mud that night without anything to . . . even the officers took off their coats to help pull the wagons.

1878 February 21st. They marched on to the scour the Kloofs and set fire to a lot of Kraals (native houses) made after the shape of a beehive on a large scale. On entering Schelm Kloofs the Kafirs commenced firing which was returned by a few volleys from the troops, a party Fingoes went through the bush and drove the enemy out, about 40 men and over 100 women were taken prisoners. But Tini Meoma their chief had got away. One of the bullock drivers had slung his hook on the way up. It was supposed that he gave information of the advance of the troops. The day was spent hunting through the bush and a shot here and there, at intervals a volley from the men. When it was getting late the Officer in command gave the order to cease fire. The Company formed up and marched to Fort Fordyce where they encamped for the night, tired and weary after their days work.

1878 February 22nd. "F" Coy patrols, guards and piquets.

1878 February 25th. "G" Coy detachment left for Shaws Farm and as soon as they got there they did not leave a hen or a chicken but they killed and roasted on fires of wood. They also robbed the orchards of all the fruit.

1878 February 26th. Piquets Guards and Patrols.

1878 February 27th. Washing clothes P.G.P.

1878 February 30th. "F" Coy sent out a fatigue party to get wood for the cooks fires, Sergt. Thompson was in charge. They went to where there was an old Kafir village, about 3 miles from camp, near the little Camboos river. Two men were placed on sentry while the others were loading the wagons with wood. One of the sentries gave the alarm that a party of the enemy was approaching. Everyone stood to his arms and seeing the number of the enemy, the Sergt. thought it advisable to retire, which they did in double time until they reached camp. Colonel Warren, commanding Diamond Field Light Horse Volunteers, as soon as he heard the news, ordered 3 troops of his men to get ready. An order which was promptly obeyed, for in 5 minutes, the volunteers were flying across country, on horseback in the direction of the enemy. After ten minutes hard ride, they came in sight of them. There seemed about 40 of them. "F" Coy, under Captain Sandham, could be seen coming from the camp, so the officer determined to wait until he came up and endeavour to surround them. The Coy. on its arrival, was thrown out in skirmishing order. The mounted men then took to the right and left to try and cut off their retreat. The movement was seen and before they could get round, they were off, not before they got a volley from the Company which laid 15 of them on the ground. There was one of them did not attempt to move and on a closer inspection it was seen he was covered with large sores, like leprosy. No man would go near him. So they left him alone in his glorey. There was some cattle taken, a few cows and 3 horses. Many men and women came into camp and as usual they got 3 days rations and sent about their business though we were well aware they belonged to the enemy.

1878 March 14th. 2 Coys. 88th Connaught Rangers relieved us at Port Wellington and we proceeded by march to Kie Road.

1878 March 15th. Went by train to King Williams Town. We arrived early in the morning and remained all night.

1878 March 16th. At 2 p.m. we marched out of town

for Fort Cox. As we were crossing the Buffalo River it commenced raining and in a minute we were soaked to the skin. We were going up a hill at the time and it was as much as we could do to keep our feet against the rush of water coming down. Some persons reading this would say it was impossible in so short a time, though anyone who was in Africa could prove the correctness of the statement. The Captain of the Company was taken off his feet by the force of the water which rose above our knees. We marched out until 8 o'clock when the order to halt and outpace. The bullocks let out to grass and a party of men sent out to gather wood to make fires and get some tea ready. When the wood was got it was rather a difficult matter to light fires as both the ground and wood was wet. It still kept raining. After some time hot water was ready and the tea thrown and with some biscuits we had to make the best of it. After two hours rest we fell in and marched to a place called Greenriver. We could not pitch tents so Captain Sandham thought it best to march all night. The mud was a foot deep on the road which made the march anything but pleasant. The men kept singing all the way and the heavier the rain fell the more they sung. Every now and then some unlucky fellow falling up to his neck in a hole of mud and water which caused a general laugh. At 3 a.m. the order was given to halt and never was an order more welcome. The bullocks were again let loose, more

fires lit and coffee and biscuits served out. The
Captain spent the two hours in trying to keep the
men from sleeping on the wet ground. Though just
before the Company fell in he was standing at one of
the fires, trying to dry his clothes. He fell off to sleep
and only for one of the men he would have fell into
the fire.

1878 March 17th. At 5 a.m. we fell in and resumed
the march and never once halted until we arrived at
Fort Cox at 4 p.m. footsore and weary, making a total
distance of 28 miles. The sun came out at 2 p.m. and
our clothes began to dry, our feet were the worse as
our boots were full of sand. After getting into camp
the tents were pitched and dinner got ready. Fort Cox
is on an elevated piece of ground, surrounded by
thick bush. with a clear space on top where the tents
were pitched ; in the rear of the camp is the remains
of an old stone fort with a few houses in ruins in the
centre. To the right rear is an old graveyard and
some old tombstones on which is inscribed the names
and officers of the 2 outs of Queens who fell there in
the old Cape war of 52–3. The hill on which the camp
is situated is nearly surrounded by a river which
runs at the foot of it. On the opposite side of the river
is the Amatolas a long range of mountains covered
with trees and shrubs affording admirable covering
for the enemy.

1878 March 18th. At 1 a.m. the Company was roused as quietly as possible. When they fell in the officer went round the ranks to see that every man had his ammunition correct. They then formed fours and marched steadily off, leaving the camp with 12 men and a Corporal (myself) to guard it. It was dark as pitch when they marched off and when they got on to the road or cart track they took to the left passing a station called Burns Hill. After marching 10 miles and crossing a river 4 times they halted at Yellowood Drift where the enemy was supposed to be driven by 2/24 Regiment. They remained there until 3 p.m. and seen nothing. At 3.30 they commenced their return. They arrived at camp at 6 p.m. tired, wet and hungry, but sleep before eating for a tired man. So they lay down on their blankets and at 10 p.m. had their dinner.

1878 March 19th. We had the day to rest, all except the orderly men who had about two miles to go for water and had to be escorted by a file of the guard each time.

1878 March 20th. Washing belts etc.

1878 March 21st. 4 men and a Lance Corpl. (myself) went with a wagon to Kirkhammahook for provisions, the company having run short. The distance was 15 miles, and through the Boonia Pass where a company of the 74th Regt. was cut up in the old Kafir War, we got in about 12 noon, there was 6 men of the 2/24th there were 2 Coys. being out with Col. Wood on 7 days patrol.

1878 March 22nd. Rejoined our Company with the provisions all right.

1878 March 23rd. Striking tents and airing the ground. Patrols etc.

1878 March 25th. Got 2 lbs. of tobacco a man. The first in the country and we were very well pleased to get it there.

1878 March 26th. 12 midnight – 1 officer, 2 sergts. 2 Corpls. and 32 men had to go down and line the road between Burns Hill and Middle Drifts as the rebel chief Sandilla was supposed to be trying to get into the Amatolas in rear of Fort Cox. They remained there until 6 a.m. when they marched up to camp after breakfast, struck tents and packed them on the wagons ready for marching. At 8 a.m. we fell in and started marching for Fort Beaufort. After about 10 miles we halted outside the town, had tea, 2 hours rest and fell in. It was dark as we marched silently through the little town of Alice. The people were looking at the doors wondering what brought the soldiers there at that time of night. We marched about 9 miles after leaving the town, we then halted. It was about 2 a.m.

1878 March 27th. After 2 hours rest we marched on for Fort Beaufort where we arrived at 11 a.m. Half the Company had blistered feet and even then the Captain wanted to continue the march. But 15 men went sick and when the doctor saw the state their feet were in he would not allow it, and when it came to the Cols. ears the Captain got a telling off for not halting at Alice for the night. Beaufort is a long straggling place with a barracks in one of the rooms of which the Company 107 strong slept on the stone floor. Some of them remarking that the bed they had the night before was softer as they preferred the earth to stone. The Colour Sergt. got drunk and was going to confine the men for not going to bed at 2 p.m.

1878 March 28th. At 8 a.m. the Company was fell in and marched to Sand Grass Farm, 12 miles, and pitched tents.

1878 March 29th. 1 Officer, 2 Sergt. 1 Corpl. (myself) and 25 men were ordered to parade at 9 a.m. and marched to Crosses Farm where they arrived at 1 p.m. after marching 9 miles, nearly all uphill. They took up their lodgings in the rooms of the farmhouse, all the farm being deserted.

1878 March 30th. Patrols. No news of other Coys.

1878 March 31st. Patrols. Orders received that "G" Coy. was at Fort Fordyce, 9 miles.

1878 April 1st. Patrols. Morning and evening.

1878 April 2nd. Patrols morning through the Schelm Kloofs. At 2 p.m. a Hottentot came running up to the camp and told the officer that his brother was shot by Kafirs in the Schelm Kloof. So there was a rush for belts and rifles and marched at once for the spot where he said his brother was lying. After proceeding about 4 miles over rock and through bushes, we came to a very thick bush and we could hear someone groaning, and 4 of us with our Officer went in and found the Hottentot lying on his side. The bullet had passed right through his body, entering above the left hip bone in rear and coming out in the right breast making a terrible wound. As we carried bandages in the left pocket of our trousers, I took mine out, tore the lint in two, one half in rear and the other in front. Then we bandaged him. Mr Heathcote, the Officer in charge gave him some brandy out of his flask. We then made a stretcher out of an old bullock hide with two long poles and carried him to Shaws Schools. By this time a messenger had been sent to Fort Fordyce for the doctor and by the time we got to the Schools, the doctor was waiting there with an ambulance wagon and an escort of "G" Coy. When he saw the man he said he would have to be carried to the fort as the jolting of the wagon would kill him, but it was all the same, as he died before they got to Fordyce. By the time we got back to camp it was quite dark.

1878 April 6th. An escort of 1 Sergt. and 12 men came in from Lurd Grass Farm with 3 wagon loads of provisions for "G" Coy. 6 men, 1 Corpl. (myself) from Crosses Farm took the wagons out to Fordyce. Remained there for the night.

1878 April 7th. Marched back to Crosses Farm.

1878 April 10th. A messenger came in with orders to march at 4 p.m. next day for Beaufort.

1878 April 11th. At 3 p.m. an escort of "G" Coy. with 2 guns of 11.7. RA arrived from Fort Fordyce. We took over the guns and the escort went. We fell in at 4 p.m. and picking up the remains of the Coy. marched on to a place called Blackwater. It then began to rain. It rained so heavy that they could not get the horses to go on. They had to inyoke them and hold their heads. The thunder and lightning was fearful. We had to stand by the guns, the water running down our backs and up to our knees. It was one of the most wretched plights I ever was in and

I've been in a few. The Officer, Mr Heathcote, sung
out turn down to the Hotel and he paid for a glass of
gin for each man. Very little we thought of rain then.
It had ceased a little and we got the horse on to the
guns and continued the march. The first salute was
through a river, in we went up to our necks in water,
holding on to the wagons to prevent us from being
carried downstream. It was very dark. After 9 miles
more we could see the lights of Beaufort and at
11 p.m. we got to the barracks. We had to lie on the
stone floor in our wet clothes and one blanket, we
could not even get a pair of dry socks to put on.

1878 April 12th. We fell in at 12 noon and marched
to Alice, 14 miles, where we arrived at 7 p.m. in very
poor spirits. Camp was pitched and we got our
dinner about 10 p.m. Nine men were prisoners for
drunk on the line of march, a serious crime in an
enemy county.

1878 April 13th. A Corpl. and 4 men of an escort
went and brought the prisoners from the guard tent
to go before the commanding officer Major Cherry.
He gave them all 28 days C.C. except 2 who he put
back for court martial. Taylor 90th. L.I. and Drvr.
Bagley R.A.

1878 April 14th. At 11 a.m. the court martial
assembled for the trial of the prisoners and the Coy.

ordered to parade as drill order at 2 p.m. About
1 p.m. one of the guns was drawn up on an open
space in front of the tents and unlimbered. At 2 p.m.
the Coy. fell in and marched to where the gun
carriage stood and with the men of the R.A. formed a
square round it. We got the command to fix bayonets
and then the escort from the guard brought in the
prisoners. The artillery man was first, tied to the
wheel and a farrier stepped to the front and took off
his coat, everyone had heard of the cat'o'nine tails, it
was then produced and the farrier prepared to inflict
the punishment. The Officer said (farrier do your
duty) and whip goes the cat in the air and then the
sharp crack as it descended on the naked back of the
unfortunate victim, and the groans that escaped him
brought tears to the eyes of more than one man
present and blanched the cheek of men who would
and did face the enemy with as little thought of fear
as if they were at a sham fight on the hill of
Aldershot. The Officers to a man turned their backs
but our orders were look to your front. After 25
lashes the prisoner was cut down and the other tied
up and the same number inflicted. He was then cut
down and both men marched to the doctors tent to
get their backs dressed. The Major made a speech to
the Coy. and they were then dismissed, cursing the
cruelty of the army at large and all commanding
officers to boot.

1878 April 15th. Parade in drill order, forming fours and skirmishing in fours and we would have to go through the bush.

1878 April 16th. Washing clothes etc.

1878 April 17th. Received order to march for Middle Drifts.

1878 April 18th. Rouse sounded at 5.30 a.m. struck tents, had breakfast and marched for Middle Drifts and at 9.30 we had our tents pitched there after marching 14 miles, the quickest done in the country.

1878 April 19th. A days rest.

1878 April 20th. Rouse sounded at 5.30 a.m. struck tents and marched for Burns Hill . We took a short cut through the bush. One of the men named Rostrick was drunk on the march, was put on one of the wagons and a man named Smith left in charge of him. The man Taylor who was flogged at Alice was drunk also and was placed under escort. The wagon on which Rostrick was upset coming down the incline, Smith and him were thrown off and the lid of the Wagon fell on Smith's leg and smashed it into jelly. A stretcher was got, and he was carried to Burns Hill and placed in the Church which was used as a hospital. Afterwards the Coy. marched in and pitched tents. Distance 4 miles.

1878 April 21st. Court martial for the trial of the two prisoners. Smith's leg was taken off below the knee.

1878 April 22nd. Another flogging match. Taylor 50 lashes and Rostrick 28 days C.C.

1878 April 27th. Rouse sounded at 5.30 p.m. Struck tents and marched to an open space of ground close to the Pirie Bush. Six men and Corpl. outlying piquets lay in the bush all night with a party of six Hottentots.

1878 April 28th. As usual, cleaning equipment etc.

1878 April 29th. At 2 pm. the camp was turned out and the Captain went round with his glasses to the men pointing out the enemy on a grass patch about 2 miles off. There was about 7–800 of them. The report was sent to Burns Hill to Major Cherry, who in the meantime arrived there with "G" and "H" Companies. An orderly was sent off to Yellowwood Drifts to "A" and "B" Coys. The order came back that the Coy. was to hold themselves in readiness at 4 a.m. the following morning, as a general atack was to be made on the bush.

1878 April 30th. At half past 3 a.m. the Colour Sergt. went round and woke up the Company. We turned out quietly and had some preserved meat and biscuits, fell in leaving our tents standing and marched silently down to the edge of the road and lay down to wait the coming of the other Companies from Burns Hill. About 4.30 a.m. the steady march of a number of men coming in that direction could be heard and shortly afterwards the Coy. passed and they thinking the "F" Company was still sleeping in their tents and some jokes were passed between them, to that effect which caused a laugh from us which made the other Coy. aware of our presence. A mounted infantry party under Mr Rawlins 90th L.I. then passed. The 2 Coys. and mounted men halted on a rise to our left for to wait until it was clear enough to push on as it was still dark. When it became clear enough to march on, the order was taking up from the leading Coy. and away we went. As we were passing the mounted men, they got the order to mount. They done so and one of them noticed his indicator at full cock. Being in the saddle, the rifle was resting on his right hip. He seized the upper part with the left hand and pressed the trigger with his right. When the rifle went off and the bullet lodged in the breast of one of his chums in front and killed him on the spot. The man was not aware that the rifle was loaded, and it was found out afterward that the man Sylvester, who was shot, was the man who loaded the rifle when he was on horse piquet, the night before and in the darkness and hurry of leaving camp in the morning the rifles were changed. The corpse was placed on a stretcher and carried down to "F" Companies camp, which was afterward called Fort Sylvester. All forts there having obtained their names in a similar manner. The Coys. then marched on to a pass going through the bush, about 8 or 10 feet wide, scarcely room for a wagon to get through. Before coming to the pass, one of the wagons was upset and half of "F" Coy. had to go back and put it on its wheels again, and then hurried off to join the remainder of the Coy. and marched on to the pass. As we were going through, the enemy was lying in the bush on each side, and as we were marching leisurely along, all at once we were saluted with a volley from both flanks and dropped on the knee at once, front rank to the right, rear rank to the left. Captain Stevens was shot in the mouth by the first volley and as Corpl. Hillard stopped to lift him, he was shot in the side. Pte. Cramb shot in the arm and breast, Pte Slowey arm, Flaherty arm, Pallet right lung. When the Captain was wounded, Lieut. Saltmarsh went to the front to take command of the Coy. He wanted "G" Company to advance another 50 yds. So he sang out (another 50 yds. "G") and the Coy. sprang to their feet to obey the command and as they turned to the right and were about to double forward, the Lieut. threw up his arm and fell back, shot through the heart. They doubled over his body to the front. The Colour Segt. ran to the front of the

Coy. and said, both your officers are shot men, but I will lead you, steady, and fire low, we will have revenge for our officers. It was difficult to see the enemy as they were sheltered by the trees, but if there was an arm or a leg exposed, there was a dozen rifles leveled at it. After an hours firing the enemy ceased fire and then we advanced through the pass, on to a clear space of ground on top of the hill, leaving our dead in the pass, lying side by side until our return. About 100 women and children came out of the bush and gave themselves up, and though we were savage enough to bayonet the lot, not a man attempted to injure them. The enemy loss was 200 dead on the ground. 1 Officer and 4 men killed, 1 officer and 7 men in need of medical aid. After getting into the open ground we had a rest and at 12 noon we took off our coats and prepared for scouring the bush in skirmishing order. They had the women and children in line in rear of us and the volunteers were going round taking all sorts of fancy beadwork from them. Some of the young women wearing nothing else but beads to cover their nakedness and being deprived of them stood before about 700 men as naked as the day they were born. It was cruel, but the men that done it were as reckless a lot as could possibly be found. But Colonel Wood put a stop to it when he heard several of our men crying shame. We were bad enough but we did not go that far. After going into the bush we shot about 30 men and took 5 women prisoners who were handed over to the Fingoes to take out of the bush. Sometime afterward we heard cries in the direction they had gone. I asked one of the Fingoes that was with us the cause of the women shouting and the black devil began grinning all over his face and gave me to understand in a most disgusting manner that the Fingo escort that we sent with them were ravishing them in the bush. I hit him in the stomach with the butt of my rifle and he wont forget the soldiers in a hurry. About 6 p.m. we came out of the bush and marched to camp, picking up our dead on the way. Lieut. Saltmarsh was conveyed to King Williams Town and buried in the cemetery. The men were buried at Burns Hill. Corpl. Hillard died 2 days afterwards from his wound and was buried there also. The prisoners were sent, under escort to K.W. Town the same evening.

1878 May 1st. An escort (myself) and 4 men went down to Burns Hill for ammunition.

1878 May 2nd. Lieut. General Thesegier with Co. Wood and staff came into camp and made a speech as to the steadiness of the Regiment the day before. It being a young Regt. and the first time under fire.

1878 May 3rd. Right half Coy. left at 6.30 a.m. for Burns Hill and as soon as we got "G" and "H" Coys, left for Yellowwood drifts. The left half Coy came

down in the afternoon and at 6 p.m. both the Coy.
and men that were left behind fell in to march to
Kirkamahook. It was soon dark and by the time we
came to the first ford we could not see 10yds ahead.
There was no good in trying to pick our steps so we
marched right through it in fours, up to our waists in
water. The water pumping out of our boots as we
marched pleasantly along in the dark. We were
beginning to feel a little warm when we heard the
rush of water and found ourselves on the bank of the
river again. Through it again we crossed it twice
more in the same march and went through the
Boonia Pass at 11 p.m. and arrived in camp at 1 a.m.
We received orders not to undress as we were for
patrols at 2.30 a.m. Pleasant with wet clothes we
said who would not be a soldier.

1878 May 4th. At 2 a.m. "A", "B" and "F" Companies
fell in, in our shirt sleeves and marched to the top of
Mount Kemp, about 9 miles, all up hill, no road. It
was about 10 a.m. when we got there and we had the
pleasure of seeing about 160 on another hill on the
other side of a valley about 2 miles across, but about
three hours march to get there. After an hours rest
the order was given to march back to camp where we
arrived at 7 p.m. and turned in tired and hungry.

1878 May 5th. At 2 a.m. the camp was roused by the
Segt. Major shouting "turn out the camp". We started

up and listened, the order was repeated "turn out the camp and fix bayonets". Then there was a rush for belts and rifles, clothes was not thought of for my part. I put on my belt and boots and took my rifle and rushed out of the tent, pulling the tent pole with me, letting the tent fall to the ground. In two minutes from the time the first command was given the men of each tent was fell in by the H.C. Officer, ready for anything in the shape of fighting, but I'm afraid it would be called a rather indecent picture if we were represented in the graphic as we stood there in our shirts. But such things are not to be looked to on active service. A coat or pair of trousers will not stop a bullet, but a rifle and ammunition will enable you to send some in front before you to your last rest. Boots are very good to put on in case of a night attack, as there may be some marching to be done and that can be done without trousers and impossible without boots, but in this case it was a false alarm. So we put up our tents and turned in to sleep again.

1878 May 6th. Rouse sounded at 5.30 a.m. The 3 Coys. fell in and marched to Brown's House, 9 miles.

1878 May 7th. Patrols morning and evening.

1878 May 8th. Camp turned out at 1.30 a.m. Fell in at 2 a.m. and marched to Goya Heights, about 9 miles on top of a hill. We got on top a little before daybreak. We then took off our coats and went out in skirmishing order. "A" and "B" left – "G" and "H" right – "F" centre. On entering the bush on the left, the enemy opened fire without doing any damage on the right. The volunteers kept up a brisk fire for some time. One of Col. Woods orderlies came down to us as a full gallop with order for "F" Coy to re-inforce the volunteers at once. Away we went at the double and as we drew near the right centre of the attack we could hear the bullets whistling over our heads, and on getting within 500 yds we opened fire so heavy that we soon silenced them in that quarter. There was a path leading between some rocks at the top of the Krantz. The volunteers made for it, Captain McNaughton leading. As he entered he was shot dead. The Corpl. sprang forward to assist him and fell dead on top of him. 4 men followed and were served in a similar manner. The volunteers then retired to consult one another as to the best means of getting their comrades and officer out. One man could only enter at a time. Just then Captain Longsdale came up with some mature troops called the Perie Fingoes and seeing how the matters stood, ordered 12 of his men to charge down and bring the bodies out. One of the Fingoes got shot but before the Kafirs had time to load again, the Fingoes were on them. As they rushed in they found a Hottentot between the rocks and with one of the Assegais they took his head off and carried it out on the point of it. It was rather strange as the Hottentots were friendly, but he was not. The only one that had gone over to the enemy. No one had any idea of the enemy losses. Ours were 6 volunteers and 1 native. At 4 p.m. we retired and pitched tents. We took only 1 blanket up with us and no clothes except what we had on and one tent for 17 men, as we were only to remain up there for 4 days. But the 4 days happened to be a month and when we washed our shirts, we had to remain at the brook until they dried, and to make it better, it was freezing at night and the sun scorching in the day time.

1878 May 16th. It was thought that in case a small party would have to be left to garrison the place, that a fort should be built. The Colonel gave an order the 2 Coys. was to be employed at the fort and 3 work at the road cutting through the bush, day about.

1878 May 23rd. The fort was finished and the Colonel came to inspect it. He was quite satisfied with the work. He called it Fort Evelyn, after himself.

1878 May 24th. At 5.30 a.m. the Coys. fell in to have a day in the bush going down Morry's Krantz to the Buffalo River and lined the bank. The 24th were working in the opposite. After lying under cover until about 5.30 p.m. the order was given to close over the right. As soon as the Coys. were together, right turn, quick march and march in file through the bush and turned up the Krantz. It was about 2 miles from the river to the top of the Krantz. It was the one McNaughton was shot in. Going up, the men in front seemed to be over the heads of the others. We had to hold on by monkey ropes to keep them from falling backward and if a stone got loose, it rattled down the path to the discomfiture of those in rear. Many of them had black shins. After an hours hard work we got on top and lay down completely done up. After an hours rest, we resumed our march to camp and lay down and though we had the hard ground for a bed and 1 blanket, we slept sound.

1878 June 2nd. "H" Coy. marched for Brown's House, en route for King Williams Town.

1878 June 3rd. Remaining followed to Brown's House.

1878 June 4th. Rouse sounded at 5.30 a.m. Tents struck and marched to Questia Drift, 10 miles, pitched tents.

1878 June 5th. Orders for one Coy. at at time to go in to fit clothes, half the men were naked, our clothes being torn off our backs going through.

1878 June 10th. Orders to the effect that Sandilla, the Geika chief, had been shot and his son Edmond had been taken prisoner. In after orders that the Regiment was to proceed by march route for Natal Colony (570 miles) as soon as possible. I was in orders to be Corpl.

1878 June 11th. Skirmishing through the bush.

1878 June 12th. "H" Coy. came out from K.W. Town and "F" received orders to go in.

1878 June 13th. "F" Coy. struck tents at 5.30 and marched to town.

1878 June 14th. Fitting clothes, boots etc.

1878 June 15th. Do = Do = Do.

1878 June 16th. Sunday, and being in town of course there was nothing done.

1878 June 17th. Fitting new helmets and very glad we were of it for the ones we had were not fit to look at.

1878 June 18th. Marched to Haynes Mill where the rest of the Coys. had marched to from Questia drift.

1878 June 19th. 1 man flogged for not answering his name when a defaulter.

1878 June 20th. Orders to march next morning for Natal.

This completes the Geika War. It is but a poor explanation of the hardships endured by men of the different Regiments engaged. In fact, it would take too much time to go into detail and require more patience that I can boast of possessing. But now our march to Natal is to be followed up, and before I begin I must say that the 90th L.I. and NB5BRA are the first European troops ever marched that part of the country.
No. 1633 Lce. Corpl. A. Guthrie
2nd Battn. S. Rifles
Cawnpore
Bengal

March to Natal of 90th L.I.
21st. June to 2nd. September 1878

1878 June 21st. Rouse sounded 5.30 a.m. Struck tents and marched to Igela, 14 miles.

1878 June 22nd. Halted, waiting on stores from K.W. Town.

1878 June 23rd. Marching orders, parade and inspection by Major Cherry to see that every man had his equipment correct.

1878 June 24th. Rouse sounded at 5.30a.m. struck tents and marched to Kie Road, 13 miles.

1878 June 25th. Halted, waiting for tailor shop, stores etc.

1878 June 26th. Rouse sounded at 5.30 a.m. Struck tents and marched to Blanes Farm, 9 miles.

1878 June 27th. Rouse sounded 3 a.m. Fires were lit between the lines so that we could see to strike tents and pack them on the wagons. We marched to Komgha, 22 miles.

1878 June 28th. Rouse sounded 4.30 a.m. Struck tents and marched to Kie River, 14 miles.

1878 June 29th. Rouse sounded at 5.30 a.m. and marched to Tolena, 10 miles and 8 of that uphill. 3 bullocks fell dead on the way up.

1878 June 30th. Halted. Washing clothes.

1878 July 1st. Rouse sounded at 5.30 a.m. Struck tents and marched to Butterworth, 14 miles. 2 men R.A. flogged after getting into camp.

1878 July 2nd. Rouse sounded at 5.30 a.m. and marched to Ibeika, 12 miles.

1878 July 3rd. Rouse sounded at 5.30 a.m. and marched to Idwtywa, 17 miles. We were served out with a lb. of flour a man, to make the most of for our next days rations.

1878 July 4th. Halted for the day.

1878 July 5th. Rouse sounded at 5.30 a.m. and marched to Ingarra, 9 miles.

1878 July 6th. Rouse sounded at 4.30 a.m. and marched to Bashee River, 13 miles.

1878 July 7th. Halt day. Washing clothes etc.

1878 July 8th. Rouse sounded at 5.a.m. and marched to Boe, 19 miles.

1878 July 9th. Halted to wash blankets.

1878 July 10th. Rouse sounded at 5.30 a.m. and marched to Gondulu, 21 miles.

1878 July 11th. Rouse sounded at 5 a.m. and marched to Umtata, 12 miles.

1878 July 12th. Halt day.

1878 July 13th. D.O. Buried a man of the R.A. who died of fever.

1878 July 14th. Halt day.

1878 July 15th. Rouse sounded at 5 a.m. and marched to Gondulula, 12 miles.

1878 July 16th. Rouse sounded at 5.30 a.m. and marched to N. Clora, 18 miles.

1878 July 17th. Rouse sounded at 5.30 a.m. and marched to Tesha River, 15 miles.

1878 July 18th. Rouse sounded at 5.30 a.m. and marched to Teena River, 11 miles.

1878 July 19th. Halted for the day to mend roads for the wagons next day.

1878 July 20th. Rouse sounded 5.30 a.m. and marched to Tohingwana, 20 miles, a very severe days march. No water to be had nearer.

1878 July 21st. Halted, washing clothes and belts.

1878 July 22nd. Rouse sounded at 5.30 a.m. and marched to St John's River, 15 miles. On coming to the river, there was a party of natives on the opposite bank. They said the soldiers could take what water they wanted, but that we must not cross it into their country (Pondoland). Our Colonel expected this all along but the column never halted a moment but marched straight through the river. The Pondos did not know what to make of the white chief for defying them. They retired about a mile from the river and we camped on the bank. About 300 natives had gathered on a hill in advance of the camp but they did not attempt to come near us. 48 men were detailed for outlying piquets but the night passed off quietly.

1878 July 23rd. Rouse sounded at 5.30 a.m. (No sign of the Pondos) and marched to Indinogwee, 15 miles. The grass for miles around the camp was on fire. We had to turn out about 12 midnight to prevent the fire getting in among the tents, which we succeeded in doing, by beating the grass with the tent bags.

1878 July 24th. Halt day, washing clothes etc.

1878 July 25th. Rouse sounded at 5.30 a.m. and marched to Currions Post, 18 miles.

1878 July 26th. Rouse sounded at 5.30 a.m. and marched to Nolengena, 14 miles.

1878 July 27th. Rouse sounded at 5.30 a.m. and marched to Nolegena Hills, 11 miles.

1878 July 28th. Rouse sounded at 5.30 a.m. and marched to Kirkstady, 14 miles. Lots of civilians came out to meet us. It was the first town to on the march. There was 3 Coys. 3rd Regt. (Buffs) stationed there marched down from Pietermaritzburg of them came out to meet to mention that the frontier passed us this morning enroute but they remained attached to during the 3 weeks we remained at

Colonel Woods and 40 mounted
back to Pondoland, as there was
talk of a chief going to rise in re
but he would not see Wood
came back as he went

1878 July 29th. Making ourselves comfortable for a week halt.

1878 August 6th. Parade in drill order for all hands marched passed.

1878 August 7th. Regimental sports, Running. Jumping. Tug of War etc. 90th won the Tug of War.

1878 August 8th. Shifted camp 2 miles from town a dead bullock being found in the river above where we got our drinking water from.

1878 August 15th. I was made a prisoner for allowing
in my tent. Put back for court martial.

1878 August 16th. Tried.

1878 August 17th. Parade. My court martial was read to Regt. Sentence. Reduced to ranks.

[Damaged page]

1878 August 18th. Received orders to march to Natal next day.

[Damaged pages]

1878 August [?] Rouse sounded at 5.30 a.m. and marched to Noname, 14 miles. Parade at 2 p.m. 1 man flogged.

1878 August [?] Rouse sounded at 5.30 a.m. and marched to Beastes Kraal, 17 miles. Several men got drunk and stole 2 cases of bottled stout and some brandy.

1878 August [?] Rouse sounded at 5.30 a.m. and marched to Keilvale, 13 miles.

1878 August [?] Rouse sounded at 5.30 a.m. and marched to Ibesi, 19 miles.

1878 August [?] Halted for day.

1878 August [?] Rouse sounded at 5.30 a.m. and marched to Winzunculna, 11 miles.

1878 August [?] Rouse sounded at 5.30 a.m. and marched to Isopo, 15 miles.

1878 August 28th. Rouse sounded at 5.30 a.m. and

marched to Lyonpontine, 17 miles. 2 men flogged there ought to have been 3.

1878 August 29th. Rouse sounded at 5.30 a.m. and marched to Winthlatin, 11 miles.

1878 August 30th. Rouse sounded at 5.30 a.m. and marched to Richmond, 15 miles. Bathing parade after camping.

1878 August 31st. Rouse sounded at 5.30 a.m. and marched to Umlass, 17 miles.

1878 September 1st. Halted to clean ourselves before going in to town next day.

1878 September 2nd. Rouse sounded at 5.30 a.m. and marched into Peitermaritzburg. Monday 12 noon 2nd September 1878.

1878 September 3rd. We got 3 days to play ourselves and do what we liked. No man was to be put in the guardroom for being drunk unless they were riotous. There was very few in camp except men on duty. All went to see the town. It's the largest in South Africa. In viewing the town from Fort Napier it seems like a large wood. You can scarcely see the tops of the houses above the trees but on going into the town you would almost fancy you were at home only for the number of blacks and the wild looking dresses of Dutch women and German.

1878 September 4th. All drunk. Nothing done.

1878 September 5th. All hands called to duty and got things squared up a bit for the Generals inspection of men and kit.

1878 September 6th. General kit inspection and parade in drill order and were put through a few movements for the General. 3 Coy. of 3rd (Buffs) were on parade.

1878 September 7th. Field day, skirmishing etc. and forming for attack. After getting home the Coys. were paid up. Any amount drunk. Several drunk are absent.

1878 September 8th. Saturday kit inspection.

1878 September 9th. Divine service 9 a.m. and walking out.

1878 September 10th. Parade in drill order.

1878 September 18th. Found the bodyguard for Sir Bartle Frier, R.A. fired 21 guns on his entrance into Government House.

1878 September 19th. "G" Coy. and band left for Utrecht at 3 p.m. Bands of 1/24 and 3rd Buffs played them out. "A" and "B" left late at night for same place.

1878 September 20th. "E" Coy. left for Utrecht.

1878 September 23rd. Sergt. I of M. Ross appointed Lieut. (Vice). Saltmarsh killed in action.

1878 November 7th. Marched into Utrecht after covering a distance of 225 miles. Major Rogers ordered each man a pint of beer. There was now 5 Coys. 90th L.I. in Utrecht. H7 R.A. also "F" Coy. at Newcastle. "C" and "D" at Luneburg. Utrecht is a small Dutch town almost surrounded by hills. It contained the base field hospital during the Zulu war.

1878 November 8th. Kit inspection 10a.m.

1878 November 10th. Church parade at 6.45 a.m.

1878 November 11th. Parade at 7 and 4. "A" Coy. ordered spring drill for one week.

1878 November 13th. Pte. Spencer tried by a district court martial and sentenced to 25 lashes for stealing a tin of condensed milk.

1878 November 15th. The Sergts. gave a ball. Some of the young ladies of Utrecht attended it.

1878 November 17th. Church parade at 6.30. Service was read in an old stores shed.

1878 November 18th. Parade 7 and 4. Sergt. Gill arrived from Luneburg.

1878 November 20th. Some natives were posted to each Coy.

1878 November 21st. 5 men R.A. flogged for drunkeness.

1878 November 27th. An escort of 1 Sergt. 1 Corpl. and 20 men under Lieut. Campbell left for the Bufflo River.

1878 December 7th. Doctor's inspection to see if men were fit for the field.

1878 December 14th. At the concert, Colonel Wood gave a lecture on Zulu warfare.

1878 December 23rd. 1/13 Regt. and "C", "D" Coy 90th L.I. arrived from Luneburg. Bread and cheese was got for them. Total strength of 1/13, 39 Sergts., 43 Corpls., 469 men.

1878 December 25th. Christmas Day. Nothing.

1878 December 26th. "E", "G" and "H" Coy marched to Battispruit.

1878 December 28th. "A" Coy. marched to Von Boynes Farm. Sergt. Lyons a prisoner for drunk on line of march.

1878 December 29th. Church parade at 7 a.m. Working party sent out to repair road.

1878 December 30th. Parade at 8 a.m. Sergt. Lyons tried by court martial. Reduced, but for gallant conduct in the old colony, he was restored to Sergt. again.

1878 December 31st. This is the last day of '78 and a long year before us. And a Zulu war to finish before we can think of a change for better, than hard ground for a bed, sleeping in our clothes every night. Butter 3/- condensed milk 2/- per tin cheese 3/- per lb. a candle 6/- and ounce of tobacco 6/- gin 1/- per glass brandy 1/- stouts 5/- and 3/- bottle of gin 10/-.

1879 January 1st. Parade at 7 a.m. for drill. "C" "D" and "F" Coy. left Utrecht for Battispruit.

1879 January 2nd. "A", "B", "C", "D" and "F" Coys

arrived at 12.30 p.m. In the evening the 1/13 L.I. and R.A. arrived also 400 Swazis (Natives). There was a heavy shower of rain. It lasted from 4 to 7 p.m.

1879 January 3rd. During the afternoon 2 troops F.L. Horse and Colonel Wood with about 200 more Swazis arrived from Utrecht. After 2 hours rest he went on to the Blood River.

1879 January 4th. Parade at 5 a.m. and marched to the Blood River. The 1/13 L/I/ left 2 Coys. to guard Barrispruit. At sunset the alarm sounded. The total strength of the column was as under.

1/13 P.A.L.I. 500 Rank and File	F.L.H. Volunteers	400	Rank and File
90th P.V.L.I. 750 ” ” ”	Mounted Infantry	30	” ” ”
11th Bde., 7th Bde. R.A. 125 ”	Durch and Natives	500	” ” ”
Total 2305 of all ranks.			

1879 January 5th. At 3 p.m. 2 troops F.L. Horse arrived.

1879 January 6th. The column crossed the Blood River taking off their trousers to do so. Being in the enemy country, a cattle piquet had to be found. Cetywayos answer is to be given today as to whether he will agree to terms or fight. The bands played "Blue Bonnets Over The Border".

1879 January 7th. The alarm sounded, the troops turned out and were dismissed again.

1879 January 8th. Very wet, Captain Laye read the duties of out post sentries to the Regiment.

1879 January 9th. At 11.30 a.m. the column paraded, and was drilled for an hour by Col. Wood. It is reported that Colonel Glynn's column consisting of 1/24 and 2/34 N5 R.A. attacked the enemy at the Tugelia, but they had to retire as the enemy was too strong.

1879 January 10th. The 2 Coys and 2 guns that were left at Battispruit came in today. A Zulu chief call Bamba with 20 men, 50 women and about 150 head of cattle came in and gave himself up. 7 Coys. 90th L.I., 6 1/13 L.I. and artillery left camp and marched 10 miles in the direction of the upper Tugela and camped for the night.

1879 January 11th. Rouse sounded at 2 a.m. marched 10 miles and out spanned. Colonel Wood advanced to a hill overlooking Rorkes Drift, taking with him 150 marks men and F.L. Horse. The reason for going in that direction of the upper, was to assist Col. Glynn in crossing the river. When he arrived there, he found they had crossed, and at once began their return march. On the way back, they captured 1200 head of cattle, 400 sheep and took 10 prisoners. It rained very heavy, some of the tents were knocked down.

1879 January 12th. Marched again back to the Blood River capturing 100 head of cattle 200 sheep and 9 horses.

1879 January 13th. Arrived at the Blood River. The Frontier Horse went out on patrol and brought 450 head of cattle to the camp. They had a skirmish with a small party of the enemy and killed 7 of them.

1879 January 14th. Orders. Any man wanted a sheep could have it for 5 shillings.

1879 January 18th. Parade for marching at 7.45 a.m. and marched to Tunghammai Drifts. F.L. Horse had another skirmish and killed about 30 Zulus, 3 of them getting wounded.

1879 January 20th. Marched to Tintias Drifts. F.L. Horse engaged with the enemy twice, killing about 170 and taking 9 prisoners.

1879 January 21st. Sergt. Jeffs and Pte. Graham got 5 pounds each for recovering the bodies of Captain Stevens and Lieut. Saltmarsh on 30th April 1878 in the heat of the action. The following appointments and promotions in orders. Col. Palme C.B., Major Cherry to be Lieut. Colonel, Captain Stevens to Bt. Major. The column crosssed the drift . After dinner, orders to carry one blanket, great-coat and 100 rounds of ammunition. Thrown up a small fort.

1879 January 22nd. The column moved out at 1 a.m. After marching about 6 miles, they scoured the hills, seeing small parties of the enemy in caves, on the hilltops. But on advance of the troops, they would disappear. The troops retired to camp.

1879 January 23rd. Halt day.

1879 January 24th. Marched out again and after going about 10 miles, they came across a large number of the enemy, between 4 and 5,000, on a hill called Zoblane. The Zulus did not seem to care for fighting, so after a couple of hours skirmishing, they retired. News arrived to Col. Wood that Col. Glynn's column, or at least, the General's column, he being with it, had been attacked, (that is the camp) and taken by the Zulus. All Europeans in camp were cut up amounting to 7–800. The remainder of the column being out on patrol with the General. When Col. Wood heard of this, he thought of his own small camp, 3 days in rear of him. He ordered a return march at once and marched night and day until he got to camp.

1879 January 25th. Marched in and joined the Lagger party. (Lagger is Dutch for fort).

1879 January 26th. Marched 9 miles carrying valises.

1879 January 27th. Umbaline expected to attack the column.

1879 January 28th. Orders to march but they were cancelled.

1879 January 31st. Marched to Kambulu Hill. 7 miles.

1879 February 1st. A Working party of 80 men were detailed to build a fort. F.L. Horse captured some cattle and set fire to Umbaline's military Kraal.

1879 February 2nd. Church parade and working at the fort.

1879 February 3rd. 4 Coy. for convoy duty to Lynns Spruits. 70 Volunteers were discharged. Their 6 months being expired.

1879 February 4th. The convoy returned to camp. Extra rations were served out to the men.

1879 February 5th. F.L. Horse went on patrol for 5 days. A Dutchman got 36 lashes for selling drink to the men.

1879 February 6th. Regiment paraded for practice.

1879 February 7th. Swazis brought in some cattle and 6 prisoners. A full account of the General's column disaster was read to the Regt. and the defence of Rorkes Drift, where 109 men kept at bay 4000 Zulus for 12 hours, killing 300 of them.

1879 February 9th. 12 months in Africa without a bed, not so bad, and what is better, no hope of getting one.

1879 February 10th. The whole of the mounted men were out on patrol.

1879 February 11th. Pte. Mack 50 lashes. 25 remitted.

[Pages missing – next entry pre-23rd February]

Went out to meet what he thought to be a small party of the enemy, but on getting closer he found that instead of a few Zulus, he had thousands to deal with, and being rather hard pressed, he sent in to camp for re-inforcements. 2 coys of the 24th were sent out. But scarcely a man was seen alive again of them 2 Coys., they were completely overwhelmed by numbers and cut to pieces, and it was over the dead bodies of those brave fellows the Zulus reached the camp. Col. Durnford was killed and also 200 of his men. When the Zulus gained the camp a general massacre took place. The soldiers fighting for their lives against terrible odds, but all to no purpose. They were butchered like dogs. Few were left to tell the story. The dead and wounded were cruelly mutilated, their bodies being ripped open with assegais. After the slaughter, the Zulus began their march to Rorkes Drift, which was garrisoned by Coy. 2/24th and as few men who managed to escape on horseback from Bandulu. They thought they would have no trouble in taking it, but they met with a warm reception. The Officer in charge having fortified the place as well as possible with sacks of mealies and biscuits boxes after keeping up a determined attack from 5 p.m. until daybreak, but the defence was as equally determined and the enemy had to retire having only succeeded in burning the hospital and killing 7 of the sick and helpless inmates and it cost them many of their able warriors to do that. For the reckless daring of a few men of the 24th several of the sick escaped. Those men have since received the Victoria Cross and what men deserved it more.

1879 February 23rd. I was admitted into hospital

with enteric fever and for 2 months was very bad. My comrades raving mad and dying all around me at one time. I was not expected to recover as I had lost my senses for 3 days.

1879 March 28th. Col. Wood and mounted of his (or Fylnn's column) had an engagement with the enemy on the Zoblaine Mountain. They were completely surrounded on top of the mountain and overpowered them. They could do nothing with the horses on the hill. Many of the men were killed in jumping over the rocks. Col. Wood had his horse shot under him, but he otherwise escaped injury. Col. Weatherly and his son, a lad of 16, were on the mountain. An eye witness says that the father had his sword drawn and was dealing death to all who came within reach, until at last he got stabbed in the back with an assegai. The boy ran to his fathers assistance and got killed on the spot. Any one who seen Col. Weatherly says he was as fine a looking man as ever was seen and as brave a soldier during the time he was with Wood's column. His wife was going about the Transvaal (with a bloke they called Gun-of Gun) as his mistress. There was a divorce suit on, but on the death of the husband, it of course was not necessary. Some people say Col. Weatherly could have escaped with some of his men but he would not go. He ordered them to take his boy but the brave lad refused to leave his father and died with him.

1879 March 29th. At 1 p.m. about 23,000 Zulus marched on the camp at Kambulu. Most of them had taken part in the victory of the day before and elated with the success they had in killing 280 white men, they determined to try their hand with the column. Col. Wood was pleased to see them coming as he hoped to have satisfaction for the men he had lost the day before. After they came within 900 yds of the lagger the 90th L.I. opened fire and it was so destructive they could not advance so they made for a ravine, opposite the position occupied by the 1/13th and managed to take the cattle lagger. 2 Coys. charged the lagger and after some time succeeded in driving them out. Major Hackett got shot through both eyes. Lieut. Bright shot in the groin and died. After 4 and 1/2 hours fighting the Zulus began to retire. The mounted men following them up. There was about 2,500 killed and it took the column 3 days to put them under ground in large dongas, covering them with earth. The British loss was 29 all ranks.

1879 May 12th. The Prince Imperial Accompanied by Lord Chelmsford and staff visited Utrecht.

1879 June 1st. Louis Napoleon, Prince Imperial of France was killed by a party of Zulus. He rode out of camp with a small party of scouts under command of Lieut. Carey and being somewhat tired, the party halted close to a mealie field. The enemy, about 40 in number, crept up to the party, and as they were about to mount and the Prince was on the point of putting his foot in the stirrup, they fired a volley in among them. The reports frightened the Prince's horse and he could not mount in time, as the rush was made, he held on by the saddle. He was dragged about 100 yds. The remainder of the party having galloped off, 2 were shot in the first volley. When the Prince seen there was nothing left for him but to sell his life as dearly as possible, he let go the saddle and drew his sword and rushed to meet the coming Zulus. But he was soon overpowered and killed. Lieut. Carey riding into camp reported the circumstances to Bdr. Wood and Col. Bullier. The latter on hearing of the Prince's death called Carey a coward and drew his revolver and had Wood not interposed he would have shot him where he stood. Wood sent Carey to his tent a prisoner. Eventually he was tried for cowardice, but by the request of the Empress Eugene, the Prince's mother, he was sentenced to be dismissed the service but since then he has been restored to the rank of Captain.

1879 July 4th. Battle of Ulundi where Lord Chelmsford met the Zulus on the open ground with about 6,000 men while the Zulu army mustered 20,000. After 40 minutes of fighting they began to waver and broke up and fled. The Dragoons and the Lancers riding after and sabring all they could come up with. The British loss was trifling compared to the enemy, where losses were estimated at 2,000. The British about 30 killed and about 90 or 100 wounded.

1879 September 10th. Marched from Utrecht to Newcastle.

1879 September 17th. Marched to Grays Farm.

1879 September 18th. Marched to Pilgrims Rest.

1879 September 19th. Marched to Paddy Careys Hotel.

1879 September 20th. Marched to Tent Hotel.

1879 September 21st. Marched into Ladysmith and halted.

1879 September 22nd. Admitted into hospital with dysentry.

1879 October 22nd. Started down country with the sick. Halted at the Rising Sun.

1879 October 23rd. Marched to the Glasgow Hotel.

1879 October 24th. Marched to Escort.

1879 October 25th. Marched to Griffith's farm and stole his geese.

1879 October 26th. Marched to the Mooi River.

1879 October 27th. Marched to Hawick or Umgeni Falls.

1879 October 28th. Marched to Pietermaritzburg and taken to the hospital there.

1879 November 9th. Discharged from hospital. My Regiment had gone to India so they had to send me home.

1879 November 13th. Marched to Camperdown.

1879 November 14th. Bothas Hill.

1879 November 15th. Marched into Pine Town where the time expired and invalids were waiting to go home. The Regt. having left for India on the 13th of October.

1879 December 30th. Went by rail from Pine Town to Durban.

1879 December 31st. Embarked on board H.M.S. *Himalaya,* our first step for home, having on board the 97th Regt. 113 90th L.I. 131 men 80th, 30th Company Engineers.

1880 January 3rd. Arrived at Simon's Bay. Remained 3 days coaling.

1880 January 6th. Steamed off for Cape Town. Landed 80th and took on 1 Coy. 91st Highlanders for St. Helena and a draft for home of the 88th Regt. (time expired). Left Cape Town same evening.

1880 January 13th. Arrived at St. Helena, landed the 91st and took on a draft of the 99th Regt. Left the same day for Ascension Island.

1880 January 16th. Arrived at Ascension Island. Remained 3 days coaling.

1880 January 19th. Left for Bermuda. Splendid weather but rather hot.

1880 February 3rd. Arrived Bermuda. Landed 99th Regt. Remained there until the 16th.

1880 February 16th. Took on the 46th Regt. for Gibralter and steamed out of harbour.

1880 February 17th. Had to return on account of some wire rope getting entangled in the fan when leaving Bermuda.

1880 February 18th. Arrived again in Bermuda. A diver went down and took the wire off.

1880 February 20th. Left again for Gibralter.

1880 February 23rd. Very severe weather.

1880 February 24th. Seas rolling mountain high. No keeping your feet on deck. No one expected to see England again.

1880 March 4th. Arrived at Gibralter at midnight. Remained 3 days. Landed 46th and 30th Coy Engineers. Took on board 71st Highlanders for Scotland and 29th Coy of Engineers for Portsmouth.

1880 March 8th. Left for Portsmouth. 3 days lost in fog and found ourselves off the Devon coast.

1880 March 13th. Arrived at Portsmouth. Disembarked the 38th men for Ireland and the Engineers for Chatham.

1880 March 16th. Left for Granton, Scotland.

1880 March 19th. Arrived off Granton. Landed 71st for Edinburgh Castle and ourselves shortly afterwards and trained it for Hamilton, where we arrived at 3 p.m. After 80 days at sea we were glad of it. I had 9 pleasant months at home, 2 months on furlough, about 6 weeks in Paisley and the remainder in Hamilton. I was happy there, but I think they reckon thats bad for service so to put a stop to it, they ordered me to India. After the usual amount of when are we to embark, when do we leave here etc., we bade our friends adieu.

PASSAGE TO INDIA

1880 December 15th. 1 Officer, 1 Sergt, 2 Corpls. and 90 men left Hamilton by the 11.30 a.m. train for Edinburgh. Arrived at 2 p.m. and embarked for London at 3.15 p.m.

1880 December 17th. Arrived in London and disembarked at 9 a.m. and marched to London Bridge Station and left by the 10.30 train for Portsmouth. Arrived at 2.30 p.m. Stood about an hour on the Quay, very cold. Embarked at 3.30 p.m. on board H.M.S. *Jurma.* (Indian troopship).

1880 December 19th. 9 months exactly from the day I landed, we left for Bombay, having on board a Battery of R.A. for Rangoon, British Burma, and drafts for the following Regiments. 2nd., 7th., 17th., 20th., 54th., 65th., 72nd., 78th and 90th. Several Officers for different other Regiments, 140 married women, about 100 children, 221 of a ships crew, making a total of 1400 persons. H.M.S. *Jurma* is 4173 tons, 371 [feet] in length, 50 in breadth 48 depth of hold.

1880 December 20th. A heavy sea running. A great many sick, especially women and children.

1880 December 21st. Stiff breeze blowing, very misty.

1880 December 22nd. Parade at 11.30 a.m. Sun shining.

1880 December 23rd. Misty, sighted several ships.

1880 December 24th. Sea calm, land on both sides, Spain and North Coast of Africa. Passed Gibralter at 9.30 a.m. about 1 and 1/2 miles on our left.

1880 December 25th. Christmas Day. No amusement of any description.

1880 December 26th. Slight breeze. Sun getting stronger.

1880 December 27th. Arrived in Malta Harbour at 5 p.m. One of the finest harbours in the world. Seen several of the 26th., 20th. and 38th Regiments who were stationed there.

1880 December 28th. Left at 4.30 p.m. for Port Said.

1880 December 29th. Splendid weather, not a ripple on the water. Sun getting stronger every day.

1880 December 30th. Cool breeze. Sun pretty warm.

1880 December 31st. Last of 1880. Sun warmer to a certain extent, sea calm. Making good headway.

1881 January 1st. At 7 a.m. arrived at Port Said on the entrance of the Suez Canal. It is inhabited by Egyptians, Greeks etc. We took on some coal and at 4 p.m. steamed up the canal.

1881 January 2nd. Still in the Suez going at the rate of 3 miles an hour. Nothing but sand on either side. The Desert of Arabia on our left and Egypt on our right. At 6 p.m. we stopped for the night. We could not go on after dark.

1881 January 3rd. At 6.30 a.m. started again and at 8 a.m. passed the town and entered the Gulf of Suez.

1881 January 4th. Calm Sea, strong sun, land to starboard.

1881 January 5th. Splendid weather, not as warm as might be expected in the Red Sea. Severe thunderstorm at 6 p.m. which lasted all night.

1881 January 6th. Heavy sea, very warm but with a slight breeze blowing which freshened towards evening and about 6.30 p.m. it rained very heavy.

1881 January 7th. Nice cool breeze. Sun very strong. About 10 a.m. passed a group of rocks called the 12 Apostles. Heavy swell.

1881 January 8th. Slight breeze, sea calm, land on port side. About 9 p.m. passed through Hell's Gates.

1881 January 9th. Stiff breeze, showery with wind dead ahead.

1881 January 10th. Splendid weather, not too hot, wind still ahead.

1881 January 11th. Heavy swells, strong breeze ahead.

1881 January 12th. Splendid weather.

1881 January 13th. Dull day. Slight breeze still ahead.

1881 January 14th. Sun rather too strong to be comfortable but we can expect nothing else in the East Indias whither we are bound.

1881 January 15th. At 10 a.m. arrived in Bombay. One of the sister troopships were there.

1881 January 16th. Disembarked at 11 a.m. in

barges and remained in the sheds until 8.45 p.m.
One party left at 7.50 p.m. for Deolali. There was
several married men with their wives belonging to
the party and when it came our turn for going, there
was 3 women came in from the town where they had
been with some of the sailors from the ship. They
began to weep when they found their party had gone
on, and seemed so innocent that strangers would be
sorry for them. But not so with us for we knew a
great deal better. So much for their first day in India
and got scarcely warm. I don't know what will be the
end of their career in India but I have a good idea
that when they have felt the effect of a hot summer,
they will conduct themselves in such a manner to be
turned out of the Regiment and sent home for
disgraceful conduct to finish up in some brothel in
Portsmouth or elsewhere. I have seen several cases
in my own Regiment during the time we were in
Africa but they were chaste and virtuous there
compared to this. The excessive heat acting like
electricity on their virtue and scattering it like the
sand on the plains of Cawnpore. When the Cawnpore
devils are in full force and poor husband is thought of
no more than if he never called her wife and I can
state from facts that women casued more trouble in
India that the heat of the country does. With my own
eyes I saw a Colour Sergt. die, shot through the
breast by his own hand over another mans wife. Men
are bad enough in this country but I heard a women

say that 3 men was not enough for one woman in the heat of the summer. We took the women with us to Deolali, very few but has heard of the Deolali Goths. It was a splendid night, the moon was full and we could see the cuttings very plain for miles around. Under and over the hills we went under 19–20 tunnels. Sometimes running along the edge of a ravine 300 or 400 feet deep.

1881 January 17th. At 4.40 a.m. arrived at Deolali, 240 miles. Some of the draft stopped in bungalows, some in marquees. Doctors inspection at 4.30 p.m. Deolali is only a rest camp for troops going out and coming home. Our link Battn., 73rd Regt. were there waiting to go home.

1881 January 18th. Parade at 10.30 a.m. for the Commandants inspection and at 8.30 p.m. 73rd left by train for Bombay.

1881 January 19th. Bathing and visiting the Bazaar.

1881 January 20th. At 4.30 p.m. left Deolali for Kandwa where we arrived at 8.30 a.m. and remained all day.

1881 January 21st. At 6.30 p.m. left Kandwa for Sohugpur where we arrived at 5 a.m. Remained there for the day.

1881 January 22nd. At 8 p.m. left Sohugpur for Jubbalpur. We arrived at 6.15 a.m. Halted for the day.

1881 January 23rd. At 4.30 p.m. left Jubbalpur for Allahabad where we arrived at 6.30 a.m. and remained for the day. Colour Sergt. Smith was there on his way home to do duty in the Depot.

1881 January 24th. At 9 p.m. left Allahabad for Dinapore where we arrived at 10 a.m. Halted for the day. Went to see the town.

1881 January 25th. At 10 p.m. left Dinapore for Mudapur where we arrived at 7 a.m. Halted for the day and changed out sea kit clothes for regimentals as we would join our Regt. next day. Sergt. Thompson was rest camp Sergt. and had his missus there with him. A beauty that required paint.

1881 January 26th. At 8 p.m. left Mudapur for Calcutta where we arrived at 7.30 a.m.

1881 January 27th. The Adjutant and Captain Heathcote met us at the station and after packing our baggage on the hackeries we marched for Fort William. The bugle band met us halfway and played us into the fort, where we were met by old comrades with a hearty shakehands, and if drinking in the canteen, we were told off. It is useful to keep an account of every days drills, etc., so I will content myself with mentioning anything unusual that may happen.

FORT WILLIAM – CALCUTTA

1881 March [?] Fort William is garrisoned by 90th L.I., 8/11 R.A., 19th M.R. Infantry. It is one of the best planned forts in the world. The inside of the fort is composed as follows. Staff barracks==Staff Officers Quarters==Royal Quarters==Single Officers Quarters==Rampart Barracks==Married and Field Officers, North Barracks==R.A. and M.R. Infantry, South Barracks==H Coy. 90th L.I. and M.R.I., Dalhousie Barracks==A.B.C.D.E.F and G Coy. 90th L.I., Queens Barracks==Married Quarter 90th and R.A. The English Church is in the very centre of the fort, and on the opposite side of the drill square from Dalhousie Bks. is the R.C. Chapel, on the right of which is the garrison library, in rear of it is the Bazaar kept by native labour, a Sergt. in charge. At the gates are guards as follows.

	O	S	C	B	MEN		C	MEN		
Calcutta Gate	1	1	1	1	15	Plassey Gate	1	3		
Chowringie Gate			1		3	Treasury Gate	Native Guard			
									C	M
St Georges Gate		1	1		6	Ater Gate	Artillery 1	6	90th	1–1–6

About 200 yds in front of each gate are two entrances

77

into the Keep, from right and left. They join at the bridge crossing the moat. The bridge is about 50 yds long, at the end of which is a drawbridge and about 5 yds from it a second.................front of each gate. The.................in half an hour it can be ......12 foot of water, by sluices..........the guns are arranged......that in 5 minutes the bridge can be blown to atoms, so that an enemy would have to swim the moat and whatever side the attack was made upon, 100 guns could be brought to bear on that point. There is said to be 100 guns in the fort but the number of men to man the fort properly is 22,000 and that number can easily be made up in case of a.................as the civilians of Calcutta..........more than half that number.................... European residents of the surrounding district would all flock to the fort. Everyone capable of bearing arms would be compelled to do so. All the buildings are flat roofed. As no fires are required, chimneys are dispensed with. The cook fires are the only ones to be seen, winter or summer. Dalhousie Bks. are the largest that I have ever seen and I very much doubt if there is another as large. 70 feet high, 100 feet wide and about 320 feet long. There are 3 rooms or flats. There are 30 steps leading to the first room at the end of which are Sergt. rooms, washhouse and baths. The men occupying the centre. 30 steps to the 2nd room and 30 to the 3rd and.................a similar number of steps to the..........by a spiral staircase which runs from the bottom to top of the buildings...........are 2 large verandahs one on each.........of these is laid out with tables ......and where the men get their meals. At each end there are two large archways leading to the stairs and 2 doors at each end leading to Sergts. rooms and 32 doors on each side leading out on the verandahs, making a total of 68 doors, and two archways to each room I need scarcely say there are no windows for the doors supply their place. Each room is capable of containing.....men. The centre of the room is nothing but pillars and arches. There are punkahs suspended from the ceiling by thin wire. It is a canvas frame about 18 inches broad and about 6 foot long and curtains hanging down to about 2 and 1/2 feet from the beds. They are attached to each other by ropes and a Coolie to every 8 punkahs who pulls them backwards and forwards from 9 a.m. to 5 p.m. and from 9p.m. to 5 a.m. for 6 pice a day or in English money 2 1/4d. They are only used in the summer and while they are at work, there is a current of cool air kept up, but the black devils sit down when the men are asleep and puts the rope between their toes and then they keep them going very slow by moving the foot backwards and forwards and finally falls asleep. It is pleasant ....of home and you...................suffocation mosquito.........eyes and ears. You can tell without opening your eyes that the punkah wallah is asleep or these mosquitos would not be there for the air

from the punkah keep them away. Besides your shirt
and drawers are wet with perspiration. You slip out
of bed cursing the black soor, take your washhand
basin and go to the tap in the verandah and fill it
with water and then steal quietly up to where the
punkah wallah is enjoying his snooze and with a
muttered curse you dash the contents of the basin in
his face and while he is blinded with water you gain
your bed shouting, kinty ton colva soor, (pull your
black   ). But the cry he gives is enough to waken
all hands and boots, brushes, pillows etc. fall round
him in showers. But water is what they dread, to spit
on him breaks....... or religion and worse than if you
stabbed him, but never saw any of our fellows do it in
fact, it is rather dangerous work, striking natives, as
you would be severely punished if brought up for it. I
am sorry to say it, but a black man is thought more
of than a white man as a soldier in this country, but
......nothing we are pretty well acquainted with the
opinions civilians entertained.........it or not they
are..........our own countrymen..........at judging a
soldier..........and those that knows least about a
soldier seem to have the strongest dislike for him. In
England, where they are more soldiers than in any
other part of the British Isles or possessions, a
soldier is thought of more than on the Plains of
Bengal, where they dont know the moment they may
have run to a soldier for protection, but well may
other countrymen treat a British soldier with

contempt when his own countrymen almost shuns the side of the street he walks upon and puts him down as a mean good for nothing scamp. There are good and bad in all grades of society, and a man, joining as a recruit, let him be of one of the best families in Great Britain, as soon as he puts on a red coat, he is treated like a dog and people shun him as if he was some wild animal, simply because he wears the Queen's uniform. The colour of his country, not that he courts their society, for before he has learned to tell one end of his rifle from the other, he has learned to look on civilians with the same contempt as they bestow on him. But speaking from experience, the generality of soldiers are manly hearted fellows and would pass the bottle to a stranger and in 5 minutes march to meet the enemy of their country. Someone must be soldiers, the country cannot do without them, and if she could not get men ready and willing to fight for their country, she would have to compell them, by passing an act to that effect and all able bodied men would have to take up arms in the defence of their homes, sweethearts, wives and little ones and many who throw slurs at a soldier might not be over willing to take his place if called upon to do so – I own, I have been ashamed to be seen in a red coat, but not for my own sake, for I care little for contempt. That dare not be expressed openly but the soldier has got the name and it will stick to him. Some truly deserving of it.

But it must be remembered that the British Army is about 200,000 strong, and must that number of men be sneered at, because of 3 or 4 scamps, here or there among them. I know, if a girl is seen in company with a soldier to say she is not good, for what reason. Simply because some girls have been with soldiers and been too obliging. Well they must put up with the consequences, I don't see how the soldier is to blame. He is a man and has the same feelings, though he has often to suffer for it in the shape of 3d per dance. For as many years as he is soldiering he must pay for his enjoyment. The inhabitants of this country, that is natives, live chiefly upon rice. A meal of rice and a good drink of water. There are different castes or religions. Some have only one meal a day some two etc. Some shave the head and leave a scalp lock hanging down in rear. Most of them paint the face, streaked or dotted, and all wear loose robes or rags for it resembles nothing else. Several yds of muslin wrapped round the body and the headdress, when any is worn, is of the same material, which is used as a covering at night by the poorer class, and is folded up and wound round the head in the day time. The women have holes bored in their nose and wear studs or rings in them, like a pig at home. Those that wear rings have them that large that they are in the way of them eating. They also wear rings on their toes, in their ears, on their fingers, armlets on their arms and anklets. They have long glossy black hair and they use a cocoa-nut oil for rubbing their skin and oiling their hair with. Those that I have seen are anything but good looking, and if they were the handsomest women in the world, the smell of cocoa-nut oil would be a damper on their beauty. But any of them dressed, in what they call European language (that is, has a dress on) they fancy themselves above the mark. The masons and bricklayers, labourers are all women. The men are very good trade............the tools they work with, but the best of it is that they do everything sitting on their hunkers, as we call it. Some of the castes burn their dead and others throw them in the Holy River (Ganges). This causes a great deal of sickness in the country and for the most part, the drainage of the town are very bad and sanitary arrangement, little or none. There are stinking ponds in all direction and the heat of the sun causes a stench to rise which is something frightful. In fact no European can stand it. There are some places in Calcutta even (the city of palaces) where you cannot go unless you are smoking and even then you are afraid to draw a deep breath. I hate all pertaining to blacks, but they must live bowing and cringing to the voice of a white man and would stab him in the back if they had the opportunity but the rule of the European in this country is, not that they are down, keep them down and anyone who has an idea how they treated the poor women and children at the mutiny, would say it was only proper.

1881 March [?] After the way they butchered them
by cutting and hacking them with knives at
Cawnpore and many other places, and in Delhi,
where 40 white women, some of them mere girls,
were taken prisoners and shut up in the King of
Delhi's Palace, there to be ravished by the Princes
and their followers and when they got tired of them,
turned them into the streets naked, to be treated in
like manner by the rabble and at length murdered in
the most brutal manner. A black man can expect
little kindness from a European who knows anything
of the mutiny or stood over the well at Cawnpore,
[Cawnpore Mutiny 21st May 1857] in the centre of
the structure erected in memory of the brave and
defenceless women and children who fell victims to
Indian cruelty. Those blacks that now almost
prostrate themselves at our feet, are the descendants
of those demons, and if they had the opportunity
they would serve us in the same manner, but if they
were left to the will of some of our British subjects it
would not be long before we'd have another
Cawnpore for they are thought far more of by the
nobility than Europeans. Those countryborn gents
who, if they were at home, would be loafing at street
corners. And as for our Anglo-Indian beauties, I could
say more than would be pleasant, as regards them
and their black servants. This is sufficient to explain.
The master wont allow a good looking (sice) groom
about his premises, and the mistress, let her be 1/2

caste, 1/4 caste or whole caste, she will take care that her Ayah (nurse) is as ugly as sin and I can assure you that is not much trouble in getting one of that description as they are all, more or less inclined to be ugly. I would never forgive the person who would think me capable of marrying a black. I am just as likely to shoot myself, but I think I can dispense with both for the present.

1881 April 18th. 90th Light Infantry paraded at 7 a.m. for the distribution of the South African Medal to the Officers and N.C. Officers and men who were engaged in the Geika and Zulu wars of 1878–9. The Coys. fell in, in quarter column. A table was placed on the reverse flank, covered with a Union Jack and several rows of chairs placed in a half circle round it to accomodate the nobility of Calcutta who wished to witness the presentation. A table was also placed on the left of each Coy. The column got the command, left turn, and each man, as his name was called, advanced his arms and marched up to the table and received his medal and returned to his place in the ranks. The officers having theirs pinned on by the General. Afterwards we trooped colours and were dismissed. There were 726 medals presented but the total number for the Regiment was 1006. The remaining 280 having either gone home, deserted or were killed by disease or bullets.

1881 May 24th. Queen's Birthday Parade in review order. Fired a *feu-de-joie* and gave 3 cheers for Her Majesty. Sun is very strong, cannot leave the bungalow from 9a.m. to 5p.m.

1881 June 30th. Suffering severely with Mango boils. A sure sign of good health, but rather uncomfortable as my body was completely covered with them.

1881 July 2nd. Admitted to hospital. I had to go at last.

1881 July 7th. Discharged from hospital, alright again. They have changed our title from 90th L.I. to Second Battalion Scottish Rifles (Cameronians).

1881 July 8th. Struck off duty and employed in Regimental gymnasium as assistant.

1881 August 10th. Same old style. In best of health. I am recommended to the Commanding Officer to be sent to pass for Gymnasium Instructor.

1881 September 17th. 8 days in hospital with fever. The Regt. amateurs played Colleen Bawn in the theatre Calcutta.

1881 October 7th. In orders to proceed to Lucknow

on the 10th to undergo a six months course of training in the Garrison gymnasium.

1881 October 10th. At 7 p.m. Lce. Corpl. McMeekin and I left for Fort William and (along with 7 or 8 chums who came to see us off) marched to Howrah station. At 8 p.m. left by train for Lucknow.

1881 October 11th. Arrived at Allahabad at 7 p.m. We only remained there 15 minutes and on to Cawnpore. 2 hours halt and started for Lucknow.

1881 October 12th. Arrived at Lucknow at 5.30 a.m. after having covered a distance of 668 1/2 miles, while we had only 2 hours halt. There was a Sergt. of the 33rd. or 1st Btn. West Riding Regiment waiting at the station to conduct us to our quarters.

1881 October 13th. Visited the Residency, Palace of Lights etc. At the Residency we visited the rooms where the women of the 32nd Regt. were kept during the seige of Lucknow and seen the room where Sir Henry Lawrence was wounded and where he died. There is a brick pillar inscribed (Landmores Post), a soldier who held his post under a heavy fire for 24 hours and as he was relieved he was shot through the breast and died. The Cantonments are about 3 miles from the city of Lucknow and is called Dilkosha. There was several cases of Cholera last month resulting in 5 deaths. It is very cold at night and hot in the daytime. The Regts. stationed there are 72nd., 33rd., 7th. and 11th. Sepoys, 10th Hussars and a Battery of R.H.A.

1881 November 1st. A few cases of Cholera. 30 men of 72nd. died. They were sent out about 5 miles Cholera dodging.

1881 December 1st. In hospital. Sprained sinew. Done climbing ropes.

1882 December 25th. Had Christmas with "G" Coy. 33rd., fared well. Got 10 days holiday.

1882 January 26th. Sports 72nd Regiment.

1882 February 1st. 72nd went under canvas prior to their leaving for Aden, which they expect to do on 7th inst.

1882 February 7th. 72nd left by rail for Deolali.

1882 February 8th. 78th Regt. arrived from Benares to take over the barracks of 72nd.

1882 February 25th. Sir Donald Stuart, Commander-In-Chief made his annual inspection and visited the gymnasium schools.

1882 March 8th. The gymnasium class are to have an assault at arms on the 9th and 11th inst. The proceed to be for the benefit of the Summer Home for Soldiers Children Masourie. A dress rehearsal is to be gone through this afternoon. The children of the Martini School are invited to attend.

1882 March 9th. Assault-at-arms.

1882 March 11th. Assault-at-arms.

1882 March 24th. Gymnasium class commenced musketry.

1882 March 29th. The Inspector of Gymnasia for India has arrived and we pass our examination tomorrow.

1882 March 30th. Passed in Gymnastics and Fencing, qualifying for First Class Certificate.

1882 April 1st. Waiting for orders to rejoin our Regiments.

1882 April 3rd. Dismissed gymnasiums.

1882 April 4th. Left by rail for Cawnpore. My Regt. in the meantime having marched up from Calcutta to Cawnpore.

1882 April 6th. Struck off duty and employed in the Regimental Gymnasium as assistant instructor.

1882 April 22nd. Received my First Class Certificate from Simla.

1882 May 10th. The Regt. paraded in full dress to have the photograph taken for the last time of 90th.

1882 June 5th. Several cases of fever, all "A" Coy. No 1 bungalow. The doctors does not know what fever it is, not one case recovered yet, out of 12, and there is likelyhood of there being more. This station is commonly called The Graveyard of India, but it is getting much healthier than it was some years back, but it is nothing but graves and graveyards. Our parade ground is over the graves of General Wheelers men. There are stones all round marked W.E. or Wheelers Entrenchment, where General Wheeler with his men were entrenched against Nani Saib and his followers. General Wheeler, being in a sad condition, he surrendered on condition that he and his followers would be allowed to embark in boats on the Ganges River to go down country. Nani Saib agreed to this arrangement and the British men, women and children were allowed to march down to the river. The rebels had some guns in position on the right of where they were to embark and as they got into the boats, opened fire on them and sunk or captured them and killed every man, woman and child. The place is called the Massacre Goths. Then there is Cawnpore Well, and House of Massacre close by, at least there is a marble cross to denote where the house stood. The night of the outbreak, there was a ball given in the house. Nani Saib was present, and one of General Wheelers daughters, having some suspicion that all was not right, got a pistol, and but for her sister, would have shot Nani Saib. She told her father of her suspicions but he only laughed at her. Eventually he was sorry he had not taken her advice and detained Nani Saib. When the rush was made, young Miss Wheeler was taken prisoner with the remainder and they were taken to the well. She stood on the edge of the well and her countrywomen dishonoured, murdered and cut to pieces and finally thrown down the well. Her sister was taken away and it was supposed and is rather doubtful that she went as the mistress of Nani Saib. She has never been heard of since. The younger sister who detested the rebels, was left to share the fate of the others, but as they were going to seize her, she threw herself down the well and was killed, preferring death to dishonour and many and many a prayer has been offered for those unfortunate women and children. The well is now built in, and in the centre is a pillar supporting a figure of mercy, life size, in white marble, with a willow wand in each hand, folded across the breast. The well is in the centre of what is called the Memorial Gardens. There is also the Memorial Church, close to the bungalows and another old church on the left of it, and in the centre of the lines is a monument in memory of a Company of men who were killed at the mutiny. One man named Murphy escaped, he was lying drunk in the washhouse. The bungalows are about a mile and a half from town. Maypur Bazaar at one end and Regimental Bazaar at the other, with long Bazaar attached for the use of the men.

1882 July 1st. We have lost about 30 men with the fever, but the men who are in hospital are recovering. It does not seem to get the same hold on them.

1882 August 4th. Admitted to hospital with a whitlow on my thumb.

1882 August 18th. Discharged from hospital. All right.

1882 September 1st. White clothes taken away to be dyed brown. No more white to be worn by troops in India.

1882 October 31st. Nothing worthy of note.

1882 November 4th. 1st Battn. West Riding Regt.

arrived here this morning enroute to Howshira. They are to march all the way, 872 miles.

1882 December 25th. Had Christmas dinner here and went on pass to Lucknow, came back on 26th.

1882 December 31st. Admitted to hospital with fever, caused from pain, the effect of a fall in the Gymnasium School Lucknow on the 26th.

1883 January 4th. Discharged from hospital.

1883 January 24th. 176 6-year men (time expired) left here by train for Deolali.

1883 February 10th. Generals Inspection. Trooped colours for the last time.

1883 February 12th. Field day under the General and chattie firing on the banks of the Ganges.

1883 March 1st. As usual, the weather is getting rather warm.

1883 March 17th. A draft of 57 men arrived at 10 a.m. in their Scottish Rifle clothes.

1883 March 18th. Paraded for first time in tartan trews and black belt.

1883 April 6th. Left Cawnpore for Allahabad by train.

1883 April 7th. Halted for the day.

1883 April 8th. Left by train for Jubbalpur at 5.30 p.m.

1883 April 9th. Arrived at 6.30 a.m. left at 4 p.m. for Kandira.

1883 April 10th. Arrived at 7.30 a.m. Left at 4.30 p.m. for Deolali.

1883 April 11th. Arrived at 6.45 a.m. at Deolali.

1883 April 27th. Left Deolali for Bombay.

1883 April 28th. Embarked on board S.S. *Clan Grant* for home.

1883 May 9th. Arrived at Suez Canal.

1883 May 11th. Arrived at Port Said. Had to remain 4 days to have new blades put on the propeller, having broken one coming through the canal.

1883 May 16th. Left Port Said.

1883 May 22nd. Called into Gibralter. Remained 8 hours and steamed off for Portsmouth.

1883 May 27th. Arrived in Portsmouth.

1883 May 28th. Disembarked and marched to new barracks Gosport and were attached to 66th or Berkshire Regiment.

1883 June 13th. Marched up to Fort Brockhurst discharge depot.

1883 June 20th. Was transferred to 1st Class Army Reserve, Hamilton District N.B.

PART 2

Andrew Guthrie Macdougall's Story

RECRUITED

War clouds were gathering once again in Europe. Britain had introduced the Military Act, requiring men to do military training when they became 20 years of age and then return to their job. However, when the balloon went up in 1939, I had not received my papers and carried on working. By this time I was going out with Cathie Bain until 1940. I had already received my medical and in March 1940 was on my way to Padgate in England for military training. I quite enjoyed it, a bit more exacting than the Boys Brigade (I was in the 93rd.). It was funny at times, some had tummies out and chests in. One or two had two left feet. How the instructor kept sane I will never know. He even lost his voice, but gradually we all improved and at the end were a fairly smart squad.

Next stop was Cranwell to learn our trade as equipment assistants. At this time, the evacuation of our troops from Dunkirk was in progress and our boys had been through a very rough time and looked it too, as some were brought into Cranwell to recover.

Three months had elapsed and Ted Clack and I

were posted south to Folkestone. I believe the aerodrome was named Hawkinge, and just across the channel we could hear the guns going full blast. A few weeks passed and our real posting came through for both of us to Horsham St Faith aerodrome near Norwich. Everything was new. Ted was in the uniform side and I was in various items such as screws, metal sheets and about 1,000 assorted items.

When we left Hawkinge aerodrome, we had our uniforms on, and it was mid summer. By the time we had arrived at Norwich we were stewed. What did the RAF do? We had to empty a coal lorry, a large one, too. The sweat rolled off us and by the time we were finished we headed straight for the showers to get rid of the coal dust.

Being near the coast, the German activity increased and as time went on became serious. Sometimes when on duty overnight, RAF trucks would roll up for refills of petrol. Quite often they had been to the coast to pick up our pilots who had been shot down. Unfortunately, in most cases they were dead.

Horsham St Faith was a Blenheim bomber aerodrome and the Germans stepped up their bombing and machine-gunning of our planes on the tarmac.

An overseas posting came through for two airmen. Ted Clack was one of them and he passed his medical. The other chap failed and Ted pleaded with me to take his place. I had a girlfriend in Glasgow and declined. This was the worst mistake I ever made. Not long after Ted had left, the bombing of the airport was increased. We spent a lot of time in the centre of the building where protection was better. However, this particular day, five of us stepped outside to see what the racket was. Just 150 yards from us a Dornier bomber was attacking our armoury building. Trying to silence our colleague on the roof where he was having a go at the plane, the pilot of the plane spotted us, circled and came straight towards us. We reached our air raid shelter and dived down the stairs in a heap. The bullets, hissing, landed on the shelter roof and the bomb he dropped hit the hangar fifty yards from us. I have never had much luck in the pools since.

At last a week's leave. A Flight Sergeant Gunston, had borrowed a pound from me, quite a sum in those days and he refused to pay up, so I arrived in Glasgow not as flush cash-wise as I had hoped to be. My timing was bad as Germany launched a colossal bombing raid on Clydebank and it was just a case of changing shelters from Norwich to Glasgow. The number of dead was never published, though most of the cemeteries in Glasgow and Clydebank had their quotas.

Not long after this leave, my overseas posting came through and whilst on leave I got engaged to my girlfriend Cathie Bain of 44 Colgrain Street,

Ruchill. Our last outing was to Hillfoot and a walk in the country. As we approached the tram to take us back to the city, I said to her, 'I expect when I come back I will find you married with two children.' She was upset but this is what happened in 1947.

Before departing from Glasgow, my fiancée and I called in to see my aunt, Mrs A Ingram of 48 Oran Street, Maryhill to show her the ring. 'Not much of an engagement is it,' she said. I was not impressed by such an ignorant comment under the circumstances, but that was her style.

Events moved fast when I returned to Norwich and I was soon on my way via Liverpool for embarkation and off we sailed to wake up next day in the Firth of Clyde. Our ship was the *Stirling Castle* fully equipped for carrying troops. First instructions were, uniforms to be kept on for three or four nights. We knew then we were heading north west. With U-boats the main concern, uniforms might have kept you alive for two minutes. On we sailed in a big arc swinging south then east to anchor off Freetown and our introduction to liquid quinine daily as we kept moving south. Two of our mates were detained in Freetown as it appeared their bodies could not cope with tropical heat. They were sent back later to the UK. On we sailed our escorts keeping us safe so far until we reached Cape Town.

We went ashore to receive a marvellous welcome from the citizens of Cape Town. We were wined and dined and entertained all the time we were there, and as we left most of us bought a bag of oranges of Jaffa size for one shilling and nine pence and tasting so good, we, in most cases, finished the bag before arriving in Bombay.

By this time, we had an idea of where we were heading for – Singapore. At peace then with no problems and nothing as yet on the horizon, we duly arrived and disembarked. The heat was difficult to cope with, and as we boarded our trucks and headed for the transit camp we compared the wartime activity we had left with the peace we were experiencing. On balance at this point of time, Singapore won hands down.

SINGAPORE

Our billets were first class though we expected to be spread around the airports quite soon. The first morning I made my way to the showers and then for a shave. I had just lathered my face and was poised with the razor when I saw standing opposite me ready to shave, a fellow worker from the same firm in Glasgow, J & A McFarlane. His name was Jimmy Shaw, one of the travellers. We could hardly believe it and he will appear later in a more serious vein.

I had a pal by this time, Eric Lawrence from Bristol and we went into the city quite often. The influx of troops appeared to upset the upper class on the civilian side – Raffles Hotel was their snob headquarters. The fact that we had come from war-torn Britain to defend if necessary this shower, left a bad taste in the mouth. Lavender Street was the sex capital for troops and Eric and I kept away from it for disease was rampant. We were stopped a few times in the street by young Singaporean girls about 16 and they were difficult to convince that we were not interested.

Our move from the transit camp was to Seletar

aerodrome but only for a few weeks as our destination was to be Pongol Swamp, hidden amongst the rubber trees for obvious reasons. The headquarter for RIMU or Radio Installation Maintenance Unit, the main base for a chain of Radar units from Singapore to Kota Baru near the northern border of Malaya. We were under canvas and had only morning parade before starting work. This went on for a couple of months and then we were back to square one.

Singapore was bombed on 8th December 1941, followed by the sinking of the *Repulse* and *Prince of Wales*. Japanese troops invaded from the north. Our troops, particularly the Argyle and Sutherland Highlanders and the Aussies, held them up but the pressure was too great, for, in addition, the Japs had infiltrated round our troops many using bicycles and paths and our retreat continued. Kuala Lumpur was evacuated and the onslaught on Singapore continued. Important, for work at our depot to continue, were goods which were lying on the docks at Singapore. Our driver had to go down and I sat on the top of his cabin with a tommy gun at the ready. We were lucky; obtained the equipment required and got back to camp safely.

By this time the Japs had control of the skies and were bombing our aerodromes at their convenience. Our flight sergeant desperately needed some oxy-acetylene cylinders which were stored at Seleter airfield in a shed. He gave me a party of six men to go over and collect them. The problem was, that the Japs were using anti-personnel bombs which explode on hitting the ground and were causing many casualties. We approached the airfield cautiously and waited for a lull in the planes arriving. You never saw a shed emptied so quickly, and we were back to camp without injury. Normally an NCO is in charge of such work but we had a sergeant who had been a few years in Singapore as a regular and was an alcoholic, who could not attend our morning parades.

Events were now reaching the really dangerous stage and the powers that be ordered the evacuation of 75% of RIMU to Java. We were kept busy packing all the equipment and when things were finalised Jimmy Shaw, previously mentioned, came and shook hands with me. We were now down to one officer and approximately nineteen men and I was the senior LAC again. We had to leave our camp and take to the road with the last Radar console. Some large houses in the area were now empty and we moved around them. Finally we arrived at the edge of Kallang airfield, having destroyed all our equipment. The Japs had landed on the island and we were issued with rifles.

The date was 13th February 1942.

We thought this is the end for us. The ack-ack guns defending the airfield had been moved to

Singapore and the Japs were nearing the airfield. At around 1pm that day a dispatch rider arrived with the information that an emergency arrangement had been made for all Radar personnel to be evacuated by steamer that night and had to be on the quay at Keppel Harbour as soon as possible. A truck duly arrived and our trek to the docks was horrendous.

Marooned on Pom Pom, 1942.

The truck had to stop numerous times as the bombs came down; each time we had to dive into the monsoon drains. The roads were littered with the dead and the dying. Arrival at the docks was no different; we were attacked on the quay repeatedly. It became so bad I was into the water and hung on to a barge as the bombs came down. By this time Eric was at the end of his tether. At last 5pm arrived. We were taken out to the *Tien Kwang*. As we sailed in the dusk, Singapore was ablaze.

Next morning we anchored in a large bay approximately 150 yards from a small island which we learned later to be Pom Pom island. We had travelled about eighty miles south of Singapore. Shortly afterwards we were joined by the *Kuala* which had about 600 passengers on board. Looking round the bay, which was really vast, we noticed a few miles away a ship which had already been attacked and appeared to be sinking. Our captain of the ship sent a lifeboat ashore with a number of RAF personnel to cut down as many branches as they could to try and camouflage the ship. This was a waste of time. Only one trip was made before the roar of planes was heard and nine of them appeared from behind the island. The *Kuala* was hit immediately and a bomb went through the deck killing four matrons. My pal Eric Lawrence and I were with our officer lying flat on the deck. When next I lifted my head, Eric was up on the banister and diving overboard. At that moment the captain of the ship shouted, 'Abandon ship, every man for himself.' I jumped up, on to the rail and overboard with my shoes on. Down I went and as I looked up the sun was shining so brightly even through the water I thought this must be a bad dream. Coming to the surface I struck out for the shore. The planes came back and machine-gunned us as we tried to reach the shore.

One of our crowd, not known to me as he was from an RAF unit stationed on a radar station in Malaya, turned on his back and shouted, 'Hey, Jock, could you get my wallet?' It had come out of his shirt pocket and was floating away.

I swam a few yards to my left, the water around me hissing with bullets, grabbed his wallet and threw it forward to him.

'Thanks, Jock,' he said.

I swam on, reaching the shore exhausted. I was helped ashore and still the planes kept up coming around. Hundreds were killed. The currents around the island were so powerful that hundreds were carried past and perished from exhaustion. We did not learn of this until a number of years later. We managed to get some shelter from large boulders. There was no sign of Eric. It was not until two days later, coming across some of our own crowd in the RAF, I enquired about Eric. They had found him further along the beach. He had caught the blast from one of the bombs and his stomach had been ripped open. He was dying; all he said was, 'My poor mother'. They covered his body with stones as it was impossible to dig graves. I never found the spot as we were bombed repeatedly for three to four days.

When I got back to Glasgow in 1945, I was able to contact his mother, not with the details, just that he was killed in action. He was the third son killed for Mrs Lawrence.

Now we were faced with survival. Pom Pom was a small island, some survivors had made their way to a sandy beach on the other side, the rest of us including most of the injured were opposite where the *Tien Kwang* was sunk. After the bombing she was still afloat so the captain went aboard, collected a few useful items and decided that the ship was finished and if left afloat would attract the bombers back, so she was sunk. All my gear was on board.

We had in command Group Captain Nunn, who was accompanied by his wife. He was detailed to remain behind in Singapore as he was in charge of the Public Works Department. Most of these people were given officer rank to ease their life style if captured by the Japanese.

Fortunately, on the second day a Dutch trader, the *Tanjong Pinang*, called in towards evening and we loaded the ship with women, children and nurses and the seriously injured. One of the few having shoes, I was able to stand on the sharp coral rock in two feet of water to pass the wounded, the women and children, my saddest part was passing a baby less than 1 year old. This effort was all in vain as none survived.

Our last meal had been breakfast on Friday morning, 13th February 1942. Now we faced more or less starvation – half a cup of water and one biscuit per day in the tropics. Nunn and his wife left on a barge in charge of Lieutenant Canty. He did so reluctantly (if you believe that you will believe anything). Nunn and his wife made it across to Padang on the west coast of Sumatra in time to get a berth on the steamer *Rosenboom*. This steamer was torpedoed by a Jap submarine four days out from Padang. We heard rumours of this sinking when we arrived about 8th March.

Back to the island, we were near the end of our tether. Our sixth day on half a cup of water and a biscuit, our only hope was a promise that four Chinese Tonkans would arrive to take us to Dabo, a town on the island of Sinkept, an area mostly under the control of the Japanese. The ships duly arrived. We had to keep out of sight below deck while the Chinese helmsman steered the ship. It was a nerve wracking journey and took ages, or so it seemed. Jap planes were heard repeatedly, but we arrived in Dabo safely. We had a real meal at last and we made up in two days what we had missed for six days.

Our rescuers were relieved by servicemen and we left at dusk in a motor boat to head for the mouth of the Indragiri river quite a few miles away. Rumour had it that Jap destroyers were anchored near the mouth and our hearts sank. But, fortune favours the not so brave; the destroyers must have moved north before we arrived and we sailed right up to a small town called Priggi Raja. This place was a nightmare.

We were huddled in a hut which after an hour became unbearable. Eaten alive by mosquitoes, we had to get out and we walked up and down till dawn, had a meal of sorts and then on to the motor boat to move up stream against a strong current to Tembilahan.

At this speed we were really losing too much time. On we went to Rengat, changed boats there and on to Ayer Moclek and finally Talock. The monsoon was feeding the river and we were stranded there for days by floods. At last we were on the move to Sawaloento and journey by train to Padang on the west coast. We were hoping that despite our losing so many days we might still get away but it was not to be. The Dutch had closed the port of Emma Haven, due in part to some escapees behaviour. Our hearts sank.

We were accommodated in the Chinese school. Colonel A G Warren visited us and put us in the picture. He was the officer in charge of the escape route. The date was 8th March and the news we were getting was not very hopeful. Whilst in the school we experienced an earthquake, a quite common occurrence in the area, and we ran out into the open. We now had time on our hands and went for walks. The natives were not friendly at all. Some did try getting away in small boats; our only hope was getting to Colombo. As the entire area north was in the hands of the Japanese that idea was abandoned.

112

The news coming in at this point of time was like a giant noose. The Japs had more or less captured Java. Their airborne troops had taken Palembang airport. The only plus was we were getting regular meals and then came the clincher; the capital, Medan, had been captured. After sorting this out, the Jap troops were heading south and would reach Padang soon. Their anticipated arrival was 17th March, St Patrick's Day. We were awake early and the Jap troops in trucks were passing the school. A more villainous crowd you would never see. What happens now? First order, everybody confined to school until they came to check how many troops were in the bag. As I said, we were in the Chinese school where a large portrait of General Chiang Kai Shek, the Chinese leader was hanging. The Jap officer took his sword, cut down the picture and stood on it. Next we were lined up and the Jap sergeant counted his catch. Colonel Warren addressed us. All he said was that we should take things calmly. Inside a few days we were marched from the school to the local jail. Our beds were the concrete floors.

PRISONER OF WAR

Our first two or three meals were soup and real bread to be replaced with rice for the next three years and five months. On my first night in the cell I was bitten by a rat in my arm pit. Two or three days later I required medical attention for tinia, a foot infection caused by my nine days on Pom Pom island. This cleared up and we settled down for how long, nobody had any idea.

Two months later, 500 of our party, myself included, paraded outside the camp to board a tram heading for Fort de Kock. One problem arose when the Japanese sergeant checked our numbers. He could only account for 499. Talk about a panic. The reason was found. Our commanding officer, Colonel Coate, an eminent Australian surgeon, had a great deal of luggage which he was keeping his eye on. A short distance from the parade, the Jap sergeant went berserk and assaulted our officer repeatedly. Eventually, we left the station on the train. That was to be our last civilised method of travel for many years after. A night's rest, then we were bundled on to trucks and set off heading north, still no wiser

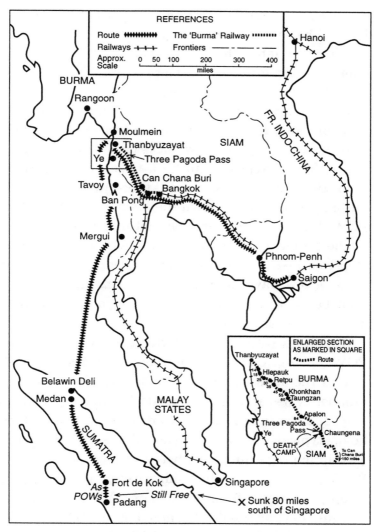

REFERENCES

Route	⫴⫴⫴⫴⫴⫴	The 'Burma' Railway	•••••••
Railways	+++	Frontiers	— · — · —

Approx. Scale

0	50	100	200	300	400

miles

BURMA

Rangoon

Moulmein
Thanbyuzayat
Ye
Three Pagoda Pass

SIAM

FR. INDO-CHINA

Hanoi

Can Chana Buri
Bangkok

Tavoy

Ban Pong

Mergui

Phnom-Penh
Saigon

ENLARGED SECTION
AS MARKED IN SQUARE
•••••• Route

Thanbyuzayat
18
25 Hlepauk
Retpu   BURMA
35
45 Khonkhan
60 Taungzan
84 Apalon
Three Pagoda
Pass   Chaungena
Ye
DEATH
CAMP   SIAM   To Can
Chana Buri
150 miles

Belawin Deli
Medan

MALAY
STATES

SUMATRA

As
POWs   Fort de Kok
Padang

Still Free

Singapore

X Sunk 80 miles
south of Singapore

Route of British (Sumatra) POW Battalion,
May 1942 to March 1945.

about our destination. Our next stop was across from Lake Toba, a most beautiful area with rolling hills. We learned later that thousands of years ago an enormous explosion took place here. The volcano exploded and the area left became the lake.

We stopped overnight at a very large house and had our usual rice meal. We noticed when we arrived that there were quite a few ducks chasing around the house. There appeared to be a dozen of them and each time they came round there was a couple missing. This went on until there were none left. The POWs had helped themselves. Nothing was said.

The following morning off we went and our last stop was Medan, quite a large city on the coast. We spent a few days here, the Dutch prisoners in this area being very good to us and we ate quite well during our short stay.

We left on 15th May 1942, this time with only 499 POWs; one of our boys was too sick to travel. This caused the Japs lots of problems when checking our numbers. We arrived at the docks and boarded a ship, the *England Maru*. Accommodation was in the hold, typical Japanese style, like sardines. This description regarding our voyages was never changed. We joined up with other ships carrying Australian troops, possibly from Singapore. We arrived at Mergui, disembarked and marched to the Mergui National High School, 499 British and approximately 1,000 Australians. Talk about overcrowding.

My bed for the time spent there was sitting on the stairs along with a few Australians with whom I got on very well. One in particular, his name Don Batey, gave me a pair of Australian boots which were a godsend to me, having lost all my kit and my shoes. The shoes I had on when swimming to Pom Pom island were showing signs of wear. We were kept busy going into town where the longest bamboo poles you could imagine were collected and carried back to our abode. Two men to one pole gives you an idea of the weight. The rumour had gone around that a new camp was being built and for once the rumour was true. Conditions at the school were atrocious. Mosquitoes everywhere and nights were sleepless, dysentery was taking its toll and it was with a sigh of relief that we moved up to our new site. The huts were well built weatherwise and bamboo poles were your mattress.

The food was drastic, especially the rice. One meal I received had rats' droppings in it. I took it down to our section boss, Chief Petty Officer Jan Tucker of the Royal Navy. 'Look Mac,' he says, 'I didn't get the extra vitamin.' It appears that the rice had come from Singapore where it had been treated, but apparently not successfully, for keeping the rats out.

The camp we were in was quite large and open, no fence around it only two strands of wire. If you were found outside, it was a death sentence. One Australian was caught. We learned later he was married with a family. I actually saw him being bundled into a truck and heading off up to the airfield, where he was made to dig his own grave and was then shot. At the same time, Don Batey, aware of the consequences was outside the wire frequently, visiting the native kampongs and bringing back medicine for the sick in hospital. No Jap was ever able to catch him.

Meantime, our first working party started work on the airfield, breaking up stones for the runway. Lots of Burmese women were engaged for this work and we were all kept very busy indeed. I had risen up to get a large stone to break up when the Jap sentry kicked me up the backside lacerating part of my thigh. I had to accept this as retaliation would have given him the chance to finish me off. The work was not particularly hard and at least helped to pass the time.

This went on for quite a few weeks until this particular day; we would work all morning and then stop for lunch. We were under strict orders not to visit any of the kampongs round the aerodrome or to mix with the natives in the kampongs. However, there is always one nut, in this case AC1 W H Coglan, Royal Air Force, who had the most magnificent black beard you ever saw. He was spotted by the Japs and a parade was immediately called. As the prisoners were all over the airfield, this took some time. Meanwhile, Don Batey had got word of what had happened and he contacted Coglan right away. Don always had his haversack with him along with his cut-throat razor and shaved Coglan as clean as a whistle. The Japs were absolutely mystified and the one who spotted Coglan received some chastisement from his sergeant in the accustomed Japanese manner.

Time passed, and then our next move. This time same accommodation by steamer further up the coast to Tavoy, disembarked, and moved about four miles to what was called the Ann Heseldine Home. This was a good move. We were actually in real wooden houses. Working parties were called for both the aerodrome and the town. I was in neither of those jobs but I cannot recall why, possibly my feet were playing up.

On 21 October 1942, we were on the move again. This time by sea to Moulmein where we spent a night in the local jail. Our march from the landing to the jail was for once a pleasure. The Burmese went out of their way to give us fruit and food which really upset the Japs.

Next morning, we were up sharp and on the road to the railway station where, as usual, we were bundled into trucks heading for Thanbyuzayat, the main railway junction for the area, and also the main hospital for the expected cases coming down from the jungle later on, as work on the railway increased. I myself, landed there about May 1943. The hospital was in name only. Bamboo beds, sheets unheard of. We spent about three days there. The highlights being an abusive speech by the Japanese Colonel Nagitoma, who stood on a table to deliver it. Muffled raspberries were our answer and off we went, heading for our first camp on what was to be the Burma Railway. This camp was at the 18 kilometre mark and was nicely situated. No fence around it and a nice stream of water a short way downhill. After settling in, the next hurdle was to sign your name more or less promising not to try and escape. Under King's Regulations we must try to escape if possible. Jock Baker and I got round that one easily. He signed my name and I his. At the same time, we had a medical check by an Australian doctor. The Aussie doctor asked me where I was born.

'Glasgow,' I replied.

'Mac,' he said, 'you have a better chance of surviving this than the rest of these blokes.' The reason was he had been trained in Edinburgh and knew all about the 'Holy City'.

The working party left early in the morning after a breakfast of rice, our staple diet all the time we were under the Japs. The railway embankment had been traced out of the jungle with bamboo poles with crossbars to where we had to dig out the soil at the side and carry it to where the level had to be made up. Normally we worked in parties of six, two digging and four carrying the soil who worked in pairs using a rice sack to carry the soil. The sack was wired at each end of the bamboo rod and then we were real coolies. Our task was measured out by the Jap guard using steel rods. Each person had to contribute to 1.2 cubic metres each. It did not remain at that amount but more of that later. Some of the embankments were nearly level, others varied, quite a lot higher.

The first week passed and we were more organised. The canteen had improved considerably and with our ten cents a day we were able to make our rice meals more palatable. Our guards were replaced by Koreans and one of our lads decided to nick off. I actually saw him walk out of the camp. Pagani was his name. I think he was Italian. The Japs went round the bend when we were one short at roll call. Amazingly, he was looked after by Burmese monks all these years and got back home a few months after we did. He had blue eyes so the habit he wore was a perfect cover.

We moved down to the 14 kilometre camp, but not for long; then it was back up to the 35 kilometre where we were joined by American prisoners under Captain Fitz-Simons. The work on the railway proceeded fast. We were now laying the rails. About 19th May 1943, we were in a camp quite a bit further on. We had only just arrived when I felt drastic. I had a stabbing pain which I thought might be my appendix. I also had malaria and dysentery. I went and saw CPO Jan Tucker and explained my problem.

I must have looked sick. He already had two very sick sailors going down to the base hospital, so we were all bundled into a truck. What a journey.

We were put in the hospital at Thanbyuzayat. A B McCaffery, Royal Navy died on 21st May. J G McAffee recovered, as did I. Later I was moved out of hospital to downstairs under the main hospital building.

I had lost quite a bit of weight and thought of a way to earn some money. I had a dutch dixie six inches in depth, around seven inches in diameter. I scrounged around and found a flat piece of wood about two feet long and four inches wide. I put strips of wood along the sides and was ready for business. I bought some native sugar from the canteen (used for feeding cattle) and wrapped it in banana leaves, one-third with water, plus the sugar and a lime. I boiled the lot over our fire. It was difficult at first to time correctly but I soon had it right. I poured it onto the board, let it set and then cut it into pieces. I tried it: great stuff; and from then on I was in business. I was kept busy and was able to supplement my rice meals with bananas etc. from the canteen.

Life moved along on an even keel until 15th June when the roar of Allied aircraft alerted me. I grabbed my dixie off the fire and was half way across to my billet when bombs were dropped about eighty yards away. I dropped to the ground but held my dixie about one foot from the ground and managed to reach my tray and pour it out without loss. Unfortunately, two of our British battalion were killed – Gunner A Rogers of 30AA and Gunner J E Shaw of 30AA who were working in this area. Not long after we were on the move back up the jungle to the 30 kilometre to join the rest of our battalion. This time we walked.

We were all quite pleased to be back with our battalion. I had accumulated a good few dollars and also regained some of the weight I had lost. At the beginning this camp was really good and interesting. Very little work was required from most of us. The death rate had slowed down though we did lose five. There was a threat to all when one of our lads contracted smallpox. I believe he was a Welshman. He was isolated and looked after by one of our medical team. It was a miracle he survived. This camp had the worst Jap officer we had ever had – a Lt. Naito. He lived on saki, a rice spirit, and was never without it. We were subject to the most ridiculous rules, restricting our use of the toilets, and walking about with a loaded revolver night and day. The cemetery was his favourite haunt and the whole camp was near a vast area of marsh and the noise of the frogs or toads was tremendous. They were enormous and the Aussies had a ball with them. They brought quite a few into the camp, each Aussie, numbering about a dozen, had his own toad. A line was drawn, bets were made and distances were marked and the money paid out to whoever owned the toad that jumped the furthest.

Chief Petty Officer Jan Tucker, myself and McAffee Royal Navy used to go along a jungle path to where there was a fair sized pool with plenty of sand. Jan would weigh about thirteen stone, myself and McAffee eight stone each. We linked arms with Jan and marched down the beach into the pool and carried on along the bottom of the pool, which was about thirteen feet deep, and up the other side. We really enjoyed this which made a break to the boring side of being a POW. We had to keep an eye on the weather each time as any fall of rain upstream resulted in a torrent sweeping through the pool and if heavy enough could be dangerous.

We eventually left this camp and moved further up the jungle. But before tackling what was to become a graveyard for forty men of our battalion – and myself nearly joining this group, I must give an account of the bridges which we built in our area of the railway. This entailed working with the Japanese engineers. Talk about slave drivers! they were the pits.

A bridge was required for every creek and they varied in height. Teak timber was used, about ten to twelve inches square at one end and tapered to a point at the other end. This was inserted into a prepared hole and a tripod erected which contained a weight approximately five hundredweight. A large number of men was used to handle the ropes in unison and it was quite effective. There were six of us at the Thailand end of the bridge and for once the Japs had hired an elephant with a mahout in charge to drag the timber up a slope, pointed end first to place in holes already dug. This proceeded smoothly until the elephant decided he wanted a break. The mahout tried to stop the elephant from getting to a nice pool of water on our side of the bridge. He was belting the elephant on the skull with the pointed iron hook on the end of his control stick. I was mad at the cruelty. We felt sickened by the evidence which covered a large area of the skull above the tusks. However, the elephant won, went into the pool and with his marvellous trunk cooled his back and sides for about ten minutes. Our relief at the elephant getting a break was short lived. The Jap grabbed six of us and we were forced to lift the teak log and carry it up the slope and place it in position. The square edge of the teak cut into the right shoulder and was painful and bruised for quite a few days after.

This was our last attempt at bridge building. By now the Japs had stopped issuing quinine tablets for malaria, using the excuse that they needed the tablets for their troops in Burma. We knew this to be a lie for the Japs had control of all the countries in which the tablets were made.

We moved steadily up to what was to be our most drastic attempt at survival, the Number 114 camp

125

not far from the three Pagoda Pass where the Burma side joined up with the Thailand side. This was quite a few thousand feet above sea level, and with very little clothing we shivered. The food was the worst so far encountered, mainly rice plus a watery soup. We were not far from the cholera camps, where F Force from Singapore was decimated.

The weeks passed and the dead mounted.

Down from our camp a short distance was a range of very tall trees inhabited by Gibbons monkeys, who have the most mournful call I have ever heard.

More weeks passed and the death toll continued to mount.

I was losing weight and suffering from malaria, beriberi and dysentery. I did not realise how sick I was when I woke up to find the medical officer and assistant had been called up from the hospital. It appeared my mate had sent for them as I was hallucinating from cerebral malaria which affects the brain. As I focused on them both, I told them no way was I going into hospital. I told them everybody that went in there was carried out dead. A week or two passed and we were moved out. Even the Japs had got the wind up. I had a job to make it up the hill to the train. I was a bag of bones and needed a walking stick (bamboo).

The journey was the usual one packed like sardines. Short of drinking water, it took ages to get down to the hospital. When I say hospital, it was no different from the usual scabby huts we were always put in. The food was a big improvement and I started to think I still have a chance to make it. I think the name of the place was Tamarkan. We were not there very long before being moved to Chunkai which was the biggest hospital we had been in so far. The man in charge, already a legend, was weary Dunlop. Also in this camp was Leo Britt, even at that time organising concerts. I saw one in the short time we were there and I was impressed by the standard. They were a great boost to our morale. After a few weeks there, we were moved back to the base hospital at Tamarkan. Whilst there I had another attack of cerebral malaria, similar to the previous one. I came to and heard the medical orderly say to the doctor, 'he has a three finger spleen'. It was not until many years later I learned the significance of that statement, which is, that malaria turns your red cells to white cells and the spleen changes them back to red cells, at the same time swelling. If the spleen bursts the white cells reaching the brain cause death.

After a few weeks the biggest move so far was on. The Japs had decided to move all the fit men to Saigon prior to being shipped to Japan to work in industries there such as coal mining etc. We were all examined by a Japanese female doctor. We lined up in our G-strings and as we bent over she pushed a glass tube with a bulb at the end up the rectum. A slight twirl and she removed it. We never heard about it being checked.

In the party for Japan were 121; 140 had died since leaving Sumatra; 196 were left at Can-Chani-Buri, to give it its full name, and there were still forty or so in the railway camps, and then the ultimate. In a few short weeks, a large party of the British battalion was sent back up the jungle to a place called Hindatu along with a similar party of Yanks; our task, to build up the embankments which were being washed away. The monsoon season was on us again and to say we were worried about surviving is putting it mildly.

The camp was 156 kilometres from base. The journey was the usual one and when we arrived what a welcome from the sandflies. Never in all our travels had we suffered so much. The scalp was their main target and the air was blue. Off we went at a rapid pace. Not many kilometres to go, a stream had to be crossed, no problem, though there could be, as the monsoon weather had started. The camp was not too bad and we settled in, both British and Yanks; no problem here, we got on well together. Inside a few days Stan Saddington, my mate, picked up a job a few miles up the railway where a Jap sergeant had a nice little job looking after hundreds of ducklings. Stan asked me to look after a big stalk of bananas, mostly green at that time though we had no idea of how long he would be away. We had a two tiered

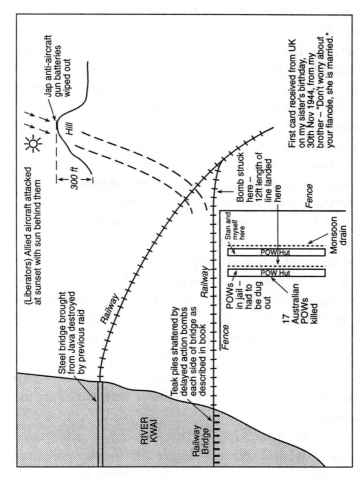

Eyewitness account of bomb attack on bridge on the River Kwai, 29th November 1944.

bunk so I tied them up. Then we were made up into working parties and each day marched to the railway to our allocated tasks, through the stream easily most times, but occasionally a bit of swimming required. The mosquitoes were as usual after their pound of flesh and those, plus the sandflies, were hell, as you would imagine. This went on for quite a number of weeks, up to our knees in mud as we battled the embankments. Stan paid us a visit and told us what his job was and a really active one it was, too. It appeared that due to the monsoon increasing its activity, the young ducks were knocked on to their backs by the torrential rain. If they were not put back on their feet quickly enough, they died. Stan's description of his dashes all round the area kept us in stitches of laughter. Eventually, the Japs gave it away and we were assembled and on the move back to – where?? We could not believe it, the Bridge on the River Kwai. We had been there before for a few weeks when we first came down from the jungle. I remembered one of the jobs I had was emptying a charcoal burner. This was a beauty; as I emerged with each log of charcoal I shivered in the noonday sun.

This time, however, the camp was mostly occupied by Australian POWs (*see* diagram). We settled in not far from the railway line which carried on over the Kwai bridge. Next hut to us were the Aussies and at the end of their hut the camp jail for the really tough

POWs. One of our crowd was in the jail. His favourite hobby was pinching. The Japs always had a sentry on duty outside the end of the hut. The first few days were quiet, then on the evening of 29th November 1944 we heard the heavy droning of aircraft approaching from the direction where the Japs had their ack-ack battery. We had a quick look and dived into the monsoon drains which ran parallel to the huts.

We had never seen such large planes – and heading now for our position. One bomb dropped on the railway line about fifty yards from our position lifted a section of railway lines, which landed in our hut twelve yards from where we crouched. Another bombed area was the next hut killing nineteen Australian POWs and covering the jail in earth. When we checked up after the planes had gone we could only find the Jap's helmet, not a trace of his body. Nobody in the jail was injured, but most had to be dug out. Our British prisoner's eyes were on stalks. Next morning, 30th November 1944, my sister's birthday, I received my first card from home after two years, eight months. It was from my brother, brief and to the point, 'Don't worry about your fiancée, she is married'.

The bombing in this area escalated and it was not long before we were on the move again. This time the rumours were true. We were all heading for Bangkok.

On the same morning I received my first card from

home, I was marched down to the bridge which had been damaged. The large steel bridge which had been brought from Java, we were told, was already down, blown to bits by a previous raid. The bridge alongside was a wooden bridge and some of the teak piles had been splintered. I was in the river bed up to my chest in water and mud and my job was to saw level the splintered ends. The Jap was panicking, as was I, for there were unexploded bombs quite near. After a couple of hours the Jap could not take it any longer and we moved back to camp.

About two or three weeks later, we were on our way to Bangkok with an overnight stop at a railway junction, and then after another boring rail journey we arrived in Bangkok, our first view of civilisation for approximately two years. We went straight down to the docks, boarded a fair sized motor launch and started crossing to the other side. The river was really broad and the current extremely rapid. One of our lads fell overboard and he was left to his fate. There was no reason why he should have gone over so the conclusion we came to was that he had had enough.

The other side was packed with large warehouses for miles. We bedded down on the concrete and our next move was marching through the town. What a sight we were. Mostly naked, except for our G-strings. Quite a number of white people, whom we thought would be French, were around. My mind is a blank for possibly one week and then we were back on the road marching to where, we did not know. We must have covered many miles with numerous stops until we arrived at a place called Kachu mountain. Our huts were nearby; the area for miles around was flat. The pinnacle referred to was where the Buddhists had their temple. Their numbers were vast and each morning they came down and went into the kampongs carrying their bowls. The people placed their offerings, mostly of an edible variety, in the bowls.

All in all we existed in three different camps in the region. One in particular caused us concern. There was only one entrance across a wide moat. This moat completely circled the camp. It was about twelve feet wide and four to five feet deep. The excavated soil was heaped on the outside level up to about six feet. No water whatsoever in it. We learned later that this was to be the site for the massacre of all POWs. At this period officers, all POWs, started to arrive in their hundreds. We settled in and soon were back to working on building an airfield, stone chipping in various sizes and fitting a gentle grading for drainage.

No 'speedo' from the Japs and surprise, surprise, there was a clump of mango trees which had to be removed and we were told we could take the fruit back to camp. There were three of us − not Macdougall, MacNab and MacKay but Macdougall,

Saddington and Lander. Harry Lander had a go first.
Up he went and lasted one minute. The tree was
alive with large red ants about an inch long. Their
nests were large with the leaves neatly put together,
possibly from their nippers. Harry was a mass of
bites. Stan Saddington went up next, same effort. My
turn, now I wanted these mangoes. I stayed up until
not one mango was left on the tree, but I suffered
then and for four weeks after. However, we got a
sackful and they lasted us for weeks. Due to the time
I had been exposed to the bites, my legs were septic.
They erupted in sores from the knee down, seventeen
on my left leg and fifteen on my right leg. I could not
go to work and pondered on what to do. I knew it
could be dangerous as I had seen so many one legged
Australians on bamboo crutches from ulcers which
could not be cured. What I tried was a shot in the
dark but it was successful in this manner. Rice is
cooked in large iron vessels called Kwalis. When the
rice is cooked and removed there is a large burnt
crust left. I removed this, broke it up and poured
boiling water into my mug. The mixture looked like
hot tea but I did not drink it. I bathed all my sores
with it. I could hardly believe it after about three
days of this treatment, the swellings started going
down and then the healing process followed. I was
back at work inside ten days. To this day fifty-three
years later I still have the scars.

The three of us carried on and then the biggest

shock of all, we were working as usual on the airfield and that evening as we came back there were two Australians who had been repairing the roof above our bed spaces and had dislodged a 12-foot king cobra, one of the most deadly of all snakes. Why? The reason was simple, it was coming down at night and helping itself to our mangoes. As they showed us the head with the poison fangs visible, our medical officer was passing by. 'Look,' he said, as he isolated the fangs, 'one nip and you're dead.'

Our next move was to a similar camp a few miles away and a complete change in the type of work required. We were to build huts for the Japanese. Unfortunately, the distance from our camp was such that we had to carry our midday meal of rice with us. Fortunately as mentioned previously, when I was making toffee in hospital, I still had my dixie. Stan only had a plate. After breakfast we collected our midday meal to take with us. A plate was no use so we collected as much as we could pack into my container to share with Stan and off we went. This work continued for quite a few weeks and the huts were getting near the finished stage.

The hut we were working on was quite large and must have been meant for the Jap headquarters. Stan and I were on the roof fitting in the roof sections of atap, i.e. leaves. We had hardly started when a Jap dispatch rider arrived on his motor cycle. He went straight to the Jap sergeant in charge of the job and delivered his message. A few minutes elapsed then we were ordered down and lined up to march back to camp (Nakhon Nie). By this time we had sensed that something important had happened and we started back to camp. We had only gone a mile or two down the road when we noticed a large party marching towards us. As we drew nearer we could see they were all officers, our own officers. As they passed they told us the war is over. We had heard this too often to believe it. We carried on up the road, quite an incline. As we got nearer to our camp and it came in view I assure you our hearts nearly stopped beating. There in the distance were the flags of our country. For me the Lion Rampant. For all of us the Union Jack. Can you imagine it? We had survived. As we got into camp the excitement increased; we were practically defying gravity.

As I sat down on the bamboo bed space the song that had sustained me through our trials and tribulations surfaced. I had taught Stan the words as near as I could remember. They were from that famous Scottish comedian, Harry Lauder and were:

> Keep right on to the end of the road,
> Keep right on to the end.
> Though the way be long,
> Let your heart beat strong,
> Keep right on round the bend.

And though you're tired and weary,
Still journey on,
Till you come to your happy abode.
Where the friends you love,
And are dreaming of,
Will be there,
At the end of the road.

LIBERATED

Now what? The place was jumping, but what do we have to celebrate with? Nothing, but not for long. Our first notable arrival, Countess Mountbatten of Burma. What a welcome she was given. Then the arrival of our planes dropping packages of food and other things we had forgotten existed. We had to keep an eye on Harry Lander. Stan and I had no idea where he had obtained his liquor but he was comatose and did not come round for ages. Stan and I took it easy as we knew our stomachs would be unable to handle the rich food etc., which appeared in abundance. Events moved swiftly as a thorough medical examination was a priority. Trucks arrived. We piled in and our first destination was Bangkok airport. From there, we left in an old Dakota, sitting with our legs in the bomb-well, bound for Rangoon. Burma is not the best country to fly over and some of the air pockets we hit and the drops we got left our stomachs in a turmoil. Still, who cares. We were on our way back.

Arriving at Rangoon we were admitted to hospital right away for check ups. First treatment was for hookworm, which most of us had through being in the jungle with bare feet most of the time. Our next stop was Bombay. Word had been sent ahead to our relatives and a letter was waiting for me addressed to RAPWI BRD WORLI BOMBAY marked to await

Author on release in Bombay, September 1945.

arrival. This was my first news from home since January 1942. My sister had married my pal Jim Findlay and they had a daughter called Andrea, which is as near as you can get to Andrew. This young lady, now 52 and with her own family, is the one responsible for me attempting to set down my war history.

Bombay was a delight and we had some lovely meals. As rice faded into the background, next thing to do was to obtain photographs to send home, which, no doubt would show a few changes. Our next move was to cross India by rail to Calcutta and stay in the grounds of Belvedere, headquarters of the RAF. We were housed in Nissen huts and provided with charpoys, a type of bed that has a stout wooden frame with four legs and stout ropes entwined corner to corner plus diagonals. I retired to bed quite late, lay down for about a minute and I was back on my feet in seconds. The ropes were full of bed bugs. After three years of this torment I was back to the same problem; we suffered on and off for about ten days.

We spent quite a few days in Calcutta, nine I believe, and were amazed at the numbers of people milling around, especially the children, so beautiful with such fine features, but the saddest part of our visit was when we crossed the 'Howrah' bridge over the Ganges river. This bridge is enormous with very wide pavements, every inch of which is fully occupied by cripples and beggars, some with self inflicted wounds. This was in 1945. Our time in Calcutta was up and we travelled back to Bombay in reserved compartments. A day or two there and a move up to Karachi, we received some pay and after a few days left by plane for Cairo. A nice flight and an aerial view of the pyramids before we touched down. Did some shopping there, mostly chocolates and fancies; greed I suppose but such a pleasant alternative to rice.

Next stop Malta. We were nearing home and the excitement mounted. How long did we stop? I have no idea, as again we boarded what was to be our last flight home. Then, our first glimpse of the white cliffs of Dover and landing at Lyneham airport. Customs ignored us and we headed for London to get a thorough medical check from the RAF. First an X-ray, then a record made of all ailments suffered whilst a POW.

HOME AGAIN

This was it at last – heading to the railway station for the journey up to Glasgow with a kit bag you could hardly get a razor blade in, so tightly was it packed. Off we went, station after station to Carlisle. What a feeling. Even as I write fifty-two years later, it floods back. At last the Central Station Glasgow. I made my way to Hope Street and waited for the No 22 blue tramcar to Lambhill. Not too long, I got in. Because of my kit bag I took a seat downstairs. The conductress was upstairs collecting the fares. Down she came. I offered my fare. 'Naw, naw, son,' she said, 'Am no taking any money from you.' I knew right away I was home.

Quite a few miles to go, then Saracen Cross and Balmore Road and my stop at Hillend Road. Off I got and tearing up the road was my brother Alastair to greet me and grab the kit bag. A few more yards and we arrived at 580 which I had left in 1941 to go overseas. My mother and sister were there. After dinner I went over to the couch to sit down. My sister Betty ran over and guided me to a chair. Just as well, my niece aged two months was lying there asleep, her name Andrea. She became the inspiration for me to write it all down now.

Later on I went for a walk down the road to Lambhill and called in to see Mrs Thom. What a welcome. Her son, my pal, Jim Thom was still in the army. I then called in to McLean's fruit shop. Gladys was there and later on the rest of the family, especially Robert who was in the RAF and before the end of the war had been flying planes from Canada to Britain. My leave was soon over and I had taken up a rehabilitation offer from the RAF which was intended to bring us back to normality.

Our destination was near Chorley and I was billeted in what had been an American camp, Washington Hall, a few miles outside Chorley. Best of all I had a companion who was with me on the Burma Railway, Johnny Hogarth. We had a great time there. I had opted for a course with the Metropolitan College, London, little realising that my eyesight had not recovered from the vitamin deficiency we had all suffered. I tried for several weeks but the task was beyond me. However, there were quite a few other interesting items which I believe were to help us back into the stream of civilisation. I joined a badminton club which had been my main sport prior to the war. I played not too badly, but far from what I had attained prior to the war.

We were now well into civvy street after being

demobbed in 1946. I called in to see my previous employer. My job was there if I wanted it. Unfortunately it was in the basement. I had been advised to be careful healthwise and I declined the offer.

Eventually at the end of 1946, I obtained a job as salesman in the SCWS Ltd, 95 Morrison Street, Glasgow. This was a very large company with 17,000 employees. I was employed in the upstairs department where the working conditions were excellent. At the beginning of 1947, a young lady started work in the department next to ours and she was to become my wife in 1949, her name Agnes Calder. This company had excellent sporting facilities and Agnes and I joined the badminton club. My health was improving all the time and I was nearly back to A1 condition.

About one month after meeting my girlfriend's parents, I had invited Agnes over to meet my mother. This required a long tram journey from Burnside to Balmore Road. I was waiting at the tram stop when who should I see across the road but my ex-fiancée with one child in a go-chair and another child aged about 4 years. I crossed over and spoke to Cathie. All I said was, 'I told you so in 1941.' She agreed. At that point the tramcar I was waiting for arrived. I could only say excuse me, and crossed over to meet my girlfriend, Agnes.

Agnes and I were now members of two badminton

clubs when we received an invitation from Bill
Jenkins of 908 Aikenhead Road, Kings Park to join
his badminton club at St Oswalds Church, Kings
Park. This team was in the fifth division and
consisted of mixed doubles. Depending on my
memory, I believe there were ten teams in each
league. Our team was:

1 Donald MacDonald and Greta McMillan
2 Andrew Macdougall and Mildred Douglas
3 Bill Jenkins and Betty Tainsh
4 Ron Harding and Freda Dunbar

Bill Jenkins was our captain, married to Thya, with
a son, Stuart, and daughter, Jacqueline. We met
regularly at Bill's house to discuss tactics. Young
Stuart kept a record of our team's results over five
years which made interesting reading as we won the
fifth division, then the fourth, third and second
division but the first division was too tough and we
finished half-way up the league. The top team was
Milngavie, pronounced Mulguy.

Years later, young Stuart became an accountant. I
previously mentioned taking a young lady, Betty
Campbell, as my guest to my first badminton club at
St Matthews. She was employed in the office of J & A
McFarlane – the same company that I worked for. On
the 11th August 1942 the company were advised by
my mother that she had received advice from the

War Office that I had died from wounds in the battle for Singapore. Later, Miss Campbell had left the company and had married a Mr Gray. We had occasion to play an away match in the Churches League. I was leading when I knocked on the door. Mrs Gray opened the door and on seeing me collapsed. She had to be taken home. I never saw her again.

In 1955, we bought a house at 736 Balmore Road, Lambhill. It was known as the Red Building and is now demolished. My wife and I knew most of the people there. All of the Thoms and Margaret and Jackie Woods whom we visited most times when we were on holiday from Australia later on. As we were now too far away from the badminton club, we gave up the game.

Meantime, I was transferred to the Head Office, Traffic Section which had a staff of twelve and dealt with all movement of freight around Scotland and also all personnel travel by air, land and sea including deputations to Canada, America and Sweden. Over time I became assistant to Mr McEwan who was in charge of the department.

After settling in I rented an area of land from British Railways on the canal bank adjacent to our building, fenced it in and started on my favourite hobby of growing chrysanthemums and tomatoes. My wife and I had a great setback when we lost our first child. Our second son arrived healthy and was christened Donald Forbes Macdougall followed later by our daughter Kirsteen Calder Macdougall.

By this time my partner, George Thom, had constructed a greenhouse to my specifications, which was five sections of four by two timber with sloping roof to a height of six feet six inches, each section to be bolted separately. Heavy duty polythene was used for obvious reasons, such as growing grosse lisse tomatoes on the hydroponic system with, parallel to the greenhouse, chrysanthemums by the name of Rayonante – a most beautiful spike variety in pink planted in a twelve foot square. The reason for this was, that instead of lifting the chrysanths into the greenhouse, the greenhouse was lifted over the chrysanths with no disturbance of the roots. By this time we were supplying the two top florists in Glasgow, who were Toni Gilmour of Renfield Street and Mary Fox of Buchanan Street. Our idea had a very satisfactory result when the Queen Mother visited Glasgow to launch a tanker on Clydeside. Toni Gilmour got the order to decorate the dais and he came in the afternoon to our place to collect the Rayonante spiked blooms. I was at work and my wife Agnes cut the number of blooms required.

A short time after this, near the end of our financial year in the SCWS I arrived in my department to be met by one of our commissioners to let me know that my boss had died of a heart attack at the weekend. We all were shocked. He had been his usual self when we stopped work on the Friday.

I was now faced with supplying the final figures for our financial year. Fortunately, my assistant, Willie Shanks, helped me considerably, and we were successful.

But before I continue, I must relate what happened when we first erected our massive greenhouse. It appeared that one of the office staff employed in the Dean of Guild's Office in George Square had seen nothing on our land when he passed by on Friday and was confronted by a sixty foot long twelve foot wide greenhouse on his way back to work on the Monday. He told his boss on arrival at work and I received a stiff letter to appear at the Dean of Guild's office immediately. I knew I had him over a barrel so I was not particularly worried. I took time off work and went along to the municipal buildings in George Square, very imposing, in fact, intimidating. Up the marble staircase I went and arrived at the Dean's office. A clerk came forward. I gave him the letter I had received.

'Well,' he said, 'do you have any explanation for building your greenhouse without permission of this office?'

I said, 'I have. I believe that before you require permission, what you build has to be a fixture.'

'Right,' he said.

'Well,' I said, 'it is not a fixture. In the summer,

tomatoes are grown. When they are harvested, the greenhouse sections are unbolted and moved over to cover the chrysanthemums for autumn flowering.'

He made a note of my explanation, took it to his boss, and when he returned said, 'As it is not a fixture, there is nothing we can do about it.'

Back at the office now and fortunately it was a quieter time until we moved into the spring. I took advantage of this and advised all our contacts on rail, air and sea of the death of Mr McEvan and that I would see them all in the near future.

Our traffic section costs for one year was over one million pounds made up of road, rail, air and sea. Each year we would have the deputations made up of directors and managers visiting the USA and Canada, sometimes accompanied by their wives, to inspect the SCWS investments in these areas of the world. Sweden was another country visited plus several others, but the biggest were the USA and Canada. On these occasions I would fly to London to be met by the gentleman in charge of London Airport, taken to his office, where we would discuss the SCWS requirements as we were very substantial customers of both (BEA) British European Airways and BOAC of overseas.

When deputations arrived back in the UK from the USA and Canada I would hire a chauffeur and Daimler limousine for a week, either to go down to Southampton for the Queen Mary liner arriving with

our party aboard or to London Airport for the
remainder. Different dates were involved and I
assisted them all through customs. One deputation,
quite a large one, kept me busy until I was left with
one director to fly back to Glasgow. This gentleman,
a Mr W Ferguson, and I duly boarded our flight and

*The first Boeing Jet to arrive in Scotland. All traffic
managers in Scotland were invited on the inaugural
flight from Glasgow to the Orkneys and back.*

everything went smoothly until we were flying over
Birmingham and, horror of horrors, I noticed smoke
was issuing from the engine on the port wing. Mr
Ferguson and I had the wind up. I facetiously
remarked we still have one engine OK. Meantime,
my wife was listening to the radio back in Glasgow.

150

She knew what plane I was on and the report was that the plane arriving from London had a problem and that the fire tenders at Glasgow airport were standing by for the arrival. You can imagine the effect this had on my wife, but the plane arrived safely.

Life moved on until an invitation arrived from British European Airways to our Secretary, Mr J Douglas, at our Head Office, 95 Morrison Street, Glasgow, requesting that I be allowed to be a guest on their inaugural flight, 8th April 1962, London to the Costa Del Sol, stopping over in Malaga until 14th April. This permission was given.

DOWN UNDER

Shortly after my return to Glasgow from Spain, Australia had launched an appeal for more migrants. I had really enjoyed the beautiful weather in Spain which reminded me of the Singapore weather without the humidity. The Glasgow papers were full of adverts and this evening when I returned home I said to my wife Agnes casually, 'Do you fancy emigrating to Australia?'

She replied, 'I would like that fine.'

We were on our way by November. My assistant was also impressed by the advert and he applied as well to emigrate.

My first step was to notify our secretary, Mr J Douglas. He was surprised, though not as surprised as I was later on, when nearer my departure date, I was invited out to dinner by the secretary and the entire board of the SCWS, and presented with a cheque.

Time rolled by. We had nominated Adelaide in South Australia as our preferred choice. Our sail date arrived, November 1962. Off we went to a Scottish farewell. One of my staff brought his pipes and we were seen off from Glasgow Central Station by friends and relations, except my mother who could not face up to our departure. The journey was reasonable and we joined our connection. My wife's brother Jack, who lived in the Midlands, was there in time to say farewell. At the docks we hastened aboard the ship *Strathmore*. Our cabin was below the waterline. We thought at the time we had been unlucky, but later on as we passed through the Bay of Biscay we realised that we were fortunate indeed as the ones up top were as sick as could be and did not get much sleep at all.

Our first call was Port Said and we got ashore to visit friends. Next stop was Colombo. My wife had to stay on board with the children. I visited some of the shops, one in particular was a jeweller's shop and I purchased a nice bracelet set with opals as a gift for my wife for missing out on that trip. This bracelet figures in my best ever purchase in Australia.

Next stop was Fremantle where the whole family got ashore, rather a strange place with straw hats worn by the men. The harbour was busy and we set off for a stroll to Kings Park. Very nice indeed and a welcome chance to stretch our legs, then all aboard for our sail across the Great Australian Bight to Port Adelaide.

It was a nice feeling to be approaching our goal. The first impact was shattering, due to the various illnesses caught by the children on the way over.

Most went into hospital to be checked. My wife had to go with them and I finished up in what was to be our home for the next fortnight. Our room had a bed but no chairs. Fortunately, my wife and Donald and Kirsteen were OK and joined me within hours. Next day we went out for a look at Adelaide. We were most impressed. What a lovely city.

Willie Shanks and his wife Agnes, plus the children were in another section. The reason being that we had signed to purchase a house on arrival.

I wrote out an application for a job giving my experience in the UK and waited for the morning paper. I spotted a vacancy I fancied and posted my letter at 7am. At 11am I got a telegram to go for an interview. I took a taxi and arrived at a large complex by the name of Brambles. My interviewer was a Lou Mercer from Springburn in Glasgow, already forty years established in the district. 'Mac', he says, 'when can you start?' He could not get over the timing of my arrival and his receiving my letter.

Within ten days, we had bought a new bungalow at Elizabeth, a new town about seventeen miles from Adelaide, but with a good train service. The house was large with all modern conveniences. I found the job quite easy and concentrated on the large garden we had both back and front. I planted out various fruit trees such as nectarines, peaches, plus grape vines. Then came a change of jobs to Woodroof Pty Ltd as paymaster. This was a large firm famous for its lemonade and I enjoyed my stay. In the meantime I had bought a car.

Quite a few of my relations had followed Agnes and me, namely my mother, sister Betty and her husband Jim Findlay plus their family of Andrea, Doris, Jeanette and Samuel. They all settled in and have done very well. I was so pleased to see my mother who could not bear to see us off from Glasgow Central Station, when we emigrated. During the summer time we would all go down to the beaches.

One day in particular my mother and I were sitting on deck chairs and enjoying the sun. She put her hand in mine and said, 'This is the best thing you and Agnes have done.' She was really happy and enjoying life. However, she was now 74 and not long after a short illness my mother died. I carried out her wishes which was cremation and the ashes to go over to the Macdougall family lair in Lambhill Cemetery, Glasgow. I made arrangements with the super-intendent and sent the casket by air. Our Lambhill friends turned up at the funeral and taped in colour the service and posted it on to us. We were overcome by such a kind gesture. In the three or four years I and my wife had been over in Scotland for a holiday I have always visited the grave and tidied up the gravestone. My father died at 50, my brother Alistair at 46. I took a while to get over my loss.

As time marched on we were really enjoying our stay. I had been reading quite a lot about the opal fields in Australia like Lightning Ridge, White Cliffs and Coober Pedy and decided at the first school holidays we would take a trip up to see the nearest one to us, which was at White Cliffs, approximately 500 miles from home. Off we went with equipment, a spade, tent, sleeping bags, etc. on our way to Broken Hill with one or two stops for refreshments. Approximately 300 miles later we were in Broken Hill. Quite an eye opener and really interesting; however, we still had at least 200 miles to go. The road was excellent though studded with dead kangaroos at intervals because of the heavy traffic. I expect night-time would cause most of it. We had approximately 100 miles of this to reach the next town, called Wilcannia, where we had a meal and then on to the last stage. This time no road but a winding track for approximately forty to fifty miles. We stopped at the store on the edge of the field, had a refreshment and then on to the opal field extending as far as the eye could see.

The first thing was to find a place to erect the tent, dig the latrines and snuggle into our beds. Next morning, the sun was up first and we had our first good view of the field. Mostly stones of all sizes, not much grass. We had noticed that when we were digging we brought up small opal chips. No value, of course, but that was to change as we gained a little knowledge each day. Quite a distance from us were pegged out opal claims with some of the miners living underground, not as you would imagine but really comfortable. We were invited during our stay to visit their quarters.

Where a claim is shown you stay clear of it, but there is such an area to explore you have no problems.

After breakfast, we had a good look round our campsite. I settled on a small patch, put down my rubber cushion and started to fossick around. Within half an hour I had found colour; in other words, a piece of real opal.

Over the years we visited other opal fields and never did I lose my love of searching. I bought an opal machine and for many years have made pendants and rings for relations and friends, but I believe the most fascinating opalised animal I ever saw was found at White Cliffs. The Aussie who found it put it in his car and travelled south many miles to civilisation to find a buyer. He was offered a derisory sum, so much so he returned to White Cliffs, staked a claim, dug out an enormous underground shelter, put in place an earth shelf. He could lay out his find, which was an opalised plesiosaur, approximately eight and a half feet long, which possibly would have lived during the time of the dinosaurs 100,000,000 years ago. We visited Andamooka but did not find it so interesting; instead of dug-outs, large bulldozers were used in 80–100 yard long swathes, each being examined for opals before another drive.

After a few years my wife and I decided to buy

some land. Our son Donald was 17 and Kirsteen 14. There was plenty of land for sale, but either the site was wrong or was not suitable, until one weekend we met a Mr Arthur Bishop and his wife and we had a chat. I mentioned our hunt for some land to build our house on and right away he said try Uley Road. We did so and found our perfect site, 800 feet above sea level. Magnificent views across the gulf to the sea in one direction, rolling hills and trees in the other, eleven acres fully fenced in, six acres level and the rest sloping down to a stream in the valley.

We sold our house and paid off the land and my wife's opal bracelet disappeared in the process. Next item was moving all our furniture on to our land for which we had built a large shed. Just prior to this we contacted a builder telling him we wanted a Spanish-type villa and we got a beauty built in record time.

I was still working in Woodroof Pty Ltd in Adelaide which meant a fair distance to travel, then one day I was in my office and one of our travellers popped in to see me. 'Mac,' he says 'there's a paymaster wanted for Munna Para District Council,' which was less than half the distance I was travelling. I applied and got the job and from then on I was in business for my favourite hobby, chrysanthemums. I ordered 5,000 in five colours and planted them out. The results were excellent, each year helped by my wife and daughter Kirsteen, we would take on average 13,000 fresh cuttings. As time passed on I acquired a Ferguson

T20 tractor and also plough and slasher. We finished up with 60,000 chrysanthemums, 200 roses and by this time we had planted 150 trees mostly acacias around the perimeter of the level land. The slope down to the burn was also planted with 3,000 radiata pines, each of which was planted by my wife and I. We would put our marking line in position from fence to fence. I would go along, insert the spade, ease it back and my wife would drop the pine seedling in and I would firm it. We would plant 500 from early morning until noon each day until our target of 3,000 was met.

During our term of eleven years on our property we had the unusual experience of a locust plague. You would have to see it to believe it. Millions of them fly down from the North. Even your car windscreen wipers could not handle it. A friend of ours went to bed at her usual time. Their property had a most beautiful lawn in front of the home. When they woke the following morning there was not one blade of grass left. Fortunately for us, it was late in our season and most blooms had been sold. Every leaf that had been left was gone, but stalks remained and we had a great crop for our last year on the property; that was in 1984.

In December of that year we had stored all our furniture at Jim and Betty's property, my sister and brother-in-law at Lyndoch in the Barossa Valley. We flew out to Scotland in time to bring in the New Year and to see my mate Jim Thom and his wife Jean. We had a marvellous year and returned to Hervey Bay in Queensland to visit our son and his wife. We bought a nice house and were able to entertain my sister and husband and his sister and husband from Hillend Road, Lambhill, Glasgow. Halley's comet was visible at this period according to the experts, and we

Author's house, Hervey Bay, Queensland.

nearly lost our eyesight trying to spot it. Our visitors saw quite a lot, this area being famous for its views and its fishing, with World Heritage Fraser Island not far from the mainland. They had a nice time and we were sorry to see them go.

My wife and I would go for walks along the beach and grassed areas at Gatakers Bay. The sunset in the evening can be spectacular. This particular evening there was a strong wind blowing and the waves were thundering in. I was so occupied I lost my usual caution regarding the grassed area. My wife shouted, 'Andrew.' I turned my head right away and there was a brown snake with its head reared ready to strike at me. I was off in a split second. This

Pelicans on the beach, Hervey Bay, Queensland.

snake is one you are warned to keep well away from due to its venom. You will recollect that was not my first encounter with snakes.

We were about eighteen months there, sold up and moved back to South Australia, stayed with my sister until we bought a house in Gawler at 1 Eucalypt drive; quite a large house in three-quarters of an acre. I had the garden full of chrysanthemums in no time.

Whilst living in Gawler a notice appeared in one of our papers stating that any ex-Jap POW who thought he might be suffering some after effects should get in touch with the Australian Veteran Affairs Department. I did so and received a letter from them with an appointment for 10.30am on the 21st September 1990 at the out-patients department Repatriation General Office. Daw pork to see Dr Minty.

I saw two people. The first I assumed was a psychiatrist, the second was Dr Minty. I was asked to relate my experiences which I have already covered. When I came to the part where my pal Eric Lawrence was killed I lost my voice and could not continue. I next saw Dr Minty who stated that I was in good physical condition. My pension was based on that interview alone, that is, three years five months on the Burma Thailand railway was not taken into account. I heard no more for quite some time until one morning I received a letter in our postbox with a cheque for approximately £5,000 sterling and a form stating that my disability amounted to 19%. Apparently 1% more would have entitled me to a pension in other words. I should have received a pension then, similar at least, to the pension granted to me in March 1996 when my latest medical check showed 40% disability due to the after affects of malaria, beriberi and dysentery.

The reader will recall that on arriving back in the UK in 1945 I was examined by a RAF doctor, had an X-ray taken which revealed that in addition to all my other illnesses I had been attacked by tuberculosis but that my system had sealed it off. I was now down to C3 classification instead of A1 when I was medically examined in Glasgow in 1940.

To crown it all, as my wife reached 60 in 1982, she received a pension of £17.76 pw in 1991. It remained at £17.76. I received at 65 in 1983 a pension of £22.14 pw. In 1991 it remained at £22.14. No need to mention who was responsible.

This was the last straw. We both had done our duty to our country. My wife in the Land Army, myself in the RAF. I decided that we would sell up, send all our goods by sea to Rothesay in the Isle of Bute in Scotland, buy a house and come back to Australia later on.

We purchased a house at 19 Crichton Road, Rothesay. As soon as we notified the pension department, we were made up right away to our entitlements as follows:

Mr A G Macdougall			Mrs A E Macdougall
from	1991	22.14	17.76
to	1991	35.50	31.25
	1992	36.50	32.55
	1993	37.82	33.70
	1994	38.82	34.50

We returned to Australia on 24th June 1994. Our pension has remained at the 4th April 1994 level since. Our costs for furniture removal were as follows:

From Gawler East to Rothesay,
Scotland   Aust $5375.00
From Rothesay to Hervey Bay,
Australia   £3563.00 sterling
                              Plus airfares out and back.

Our stay in Rothesay was a trek down memory lane. We spent our honeymoon there in 1949, the people as always, so helpful and friendly. The name of the island is Bute. Is it not strange that perfection in the Australian tongue is beaut? a delightful coincidence. We had a marvellous three years there. The scenery from any point is magnificent with the crown going to the view from the ninth tee on the golf course. High up on the hill with a view finder, my favourite view was looking towards Arran. There are no words in the English language which can do justice to this picture.

Family-wise, our son Donald Forbes is now manager, purchasing and supply for TAFE College, Maryborough. His wife Elaine is the nicest daughter-in-law anyone could wish for. Brodie, our grandson, is so like his grandad and our granddaughter, Brittany, is going on 6 but actually nearer 12.

Our daughter, Kirsteen Calder, is now divorced. Her son, Andrew, is keen on soccer. Kirsteen herself, from an early age had a thirst for knowledge and I list her qualifications as follows:

B BUS	Bachelor of Business (Admin MGNT)
DIP IPSA	Diploma Institute of Professional Secretaries
AMM	Australia Institute of Management Member
MIPS	Member of Institute of Professional Secretaries

Now Executive Officer Information Industry Training Advisory Body South Australia.

Our house is on the market as we will move back to Adelaide in South Australia where we first started off in 1963. My wife and I love the city of churches.

APPENDIX 1

U.S.A. and Canadian Deputation
September, 1961
    Mr. T. Taylor, Director
    Mr. W. W. Ferguson, Director
    Mr. E. B. Brown, Manager
    Mr. J. Wands, Manager
    Mr. C. S. Miller, Manager
    Mr. H. Y. Stewart, Manager
    Mrs. Taylor
    Mrs. Wands

All timings given in this itinerary are in local time. Local time in Great Britain is one hour in advance of Greenwich Mean Time.

E.S.T. = Eastern Standard Time = 5 hours slow of G.M.T.
E.D.T. =   "   Daylight   "   = 4   "   "   "   "
C.D.T. = Central   "   "   = 5   "   "   "   "

MR. T. TAYLOR, DIRECTOR.
MRS. TAYLOR.

Sunday 10.09.61	Flight BA 537
Leave Glasgow, Prestwick Airport	12.05 hrs.
Due New York	14.10 hrs.

    Own hotel arrangements from 10th to 12th September inclusive.

    At least 6 hours before your departure you must contact the offices of the United Airlines at Eastside Terminal, 37th Street and 1st Avenue Telephone No. TN-7-3000 to reconfirm your reservation, time and reporting place for the following flight.

APPENDIX 1

Wednesday 13.9.61   Flight UA 235
   Leave New York   12.00 hrs.
   Due Buffalo   13.22 hrs.
      Double room with bath reserved night of 13th
      September at Brock Hotel, Niagara Falls.
      At least 6 hours before your departure you must
      contact the offices of the American Airlines at the
      Statler Hilton Hotel lobby – Telephone No. TL 3-4242
      to reconfirm your reservation, time and reporting place
      for the following flight.

Thursday 14.9.61   Flight AA 407
   Leave Buffalo   15.05 hrs
   Due Toronto   15.37 hrs.
      Double room with bath reserved night of 14th
      September at Royal York Hotel.
      At least 6 hours before your departure you must
      contact the offices of the Trans Canada Airlines in the
      lobby of your hotel to reconfirm your reservation, time
      and reporting place for the following flight.
      You will meet Mr. W.W. Ferguson, Director, and Mr.
      E.B. Brown, Manager, in Toronto.

MR. W. W. FERGUSON, DIRECTOR.
MR. E. B. BROWN, MANAGER.

Sunday 10.9.61   Flight TC 855
   Leave Glasgow, Prestwick Airport   20.25 hrs.
   Due Montreal   23.05 hrs.
      Two single rooms with bath reserved nights of 10th,
      11th and 12th September inclusive at Queen Elizabeth
      Hotel.
      At least 6 hours before your departure you must
      contact the Trans Canada Airlines in the lobby of your
      hotel to reconfirm your reservation, time and reporting
      place for the following flight.

Wednesday 13.9.61   Flight TC 363
   Leave Montreal   18.10 hrs.
   Due Toronto   19.40 hrs.
      Two single rooms with bath reserved nights of 13th

and 14th September at Royal York Hotel where you
will be joined by Mr. & Mrs. Taylor on Thursday, 14th
September.

At least 6 hours before your departure you must
contact the offices or the Trans Canada Airlines in the
lobby of your hotel to reconfirm your reservation, time
and reporting place for the following flight.

MR. T. TAYLOR, DIRECTOR.
MR. W. W. FERGUSON, DIRECTOR
MRS. TAYLOR
MR. E. B. BROWN, MANAGER

Friday 15.9.61   Flight TC 851
    Leave Toronto   18.20 hrs.
    Due Winnipeg   19.40 hrs.
        Mr. & Mrs. Taylor   Double room reserved with bath
                             nights of 15th to 18th September
                             inclusive at Fort Garry Hotel.
        Mr. W. W. Ferguson
        and Mr. E. B. Brown Two single rooms reserved with
                             bath nights of 15th to 19th
                             September inclusive at Fort
                             Garry Hotel.

At least 6 hours before your departure you must
contact the offices of the North West Airlines at 404
Main Street, Telephone No. Spruce 4-4438 to reconfirm
your reservation, time and reporting place for the
following flight.

MR. T. TAYLOR, DIRECTOR
MRS. TAYLOR

Tuesday 19.9.61   Flight NW 224
    Leave Winnipeg   12.55 hrs.
    Due Minneapolis   14.20 hrs.
        Own hotel arrangements nights of 13th and 20th
        September.
        At least 6 hours before your departure you must

APPENDIX 1

contact the offices of the North West Airlines at Rand
Tower 6th and Marquette – Telephone No. Parkway 1-
3511 to reconfirm your reservation, time and reporting
place for the following flight.

Thursday 21.9.61	Flight NW 422
Leave Minneapolis	11.05 hrs.
Due Chicago	13.40 hrs.

Double room with bath reserved nights of 21st to 25th
September at Palmers House Hotel.
Mr. & Mrs. Taylor will be met in Chicago by Mr.
Ferguson and Mr. Brown on Saturday, 23rd September
and by Mr. Wands and Mr. Miller on Thursday, 21st
September.

MR. W. W. FERGUSON, DIRECTOR
MR. E. B. BROWN, MANAGER

Wednesday 20.9.61	Flight NW 224
Leave Winnipeg	12.55 hrs.
Due Minneapolis	14.20 hrs.

Two single rooms with bath reserved night of 20th
September at Leamington Hotel.
At least 6 hours before your departure you must
contact the offices of the B.N.F. Airlines 636 Marquette
Avenue, Telephone Taylor 7-2531 to reconfirm your
reservation, time and reporting place for the following
flight.

Thursday 21.9.61	Flight BN 329
Leave Minneapolis	12.15 hrs.
Due Kansas	15.10 hrs.

Two single rooms with bath reserved nights of 21st
and 22nd September at Muehlebach Hotel.
At least 6 hours before your departure you must
contact the offices of the T.W. Airlines in the lobby of
your hotel to reconfirm your reservation, time and
reporting place for the following flight.

Saturday 23.9.61	Flight TW 114
Leave Kansas	08.55 hrs.
Due Chicago	11.00 hrs.

169

Two single rooms with bath reserved nights of 23rd to
25th September inclusive at Palmers House Hotel.
Mr. W. W. Ferguson and Mr. E. B. Brown meet Mr. &
Mrs. Taylor and Messrs. J. Wands and C. S. Miller.

MR. J. WANDS, MANAGER
MRS. WANDS,
MR. C. S. MILLER, MANAGER
Wednesday 13.9.61
    Leave Glasgow Central   8.30 a.m.
        1st Class Seats No. 18 Back
        and Facing and No. 17 Facing
        Engine reserved in Coach A.5.
    Due London Euston   3.35 p.m.
        Own hotel arrangements in London for night of 13th
        September.
Thursday 14.9.61
    Leave London, Waterloo Station   10.43 a.m.
        1st Class Pullman Seats Nos.
    5, 6 and 8 reserved in Coach H
    Due Southampton Docks Station
        On arrival at Southampton, pass through Immigration
        and Customs and board Queen Elizabeth sailing at
        1.30 p.m.
        Mr. & Mrs. J. Wands – 1st Class double room No. B.28
        reserved.
        Mr. C. S. Miller – 1st Class single room No. B.47
        reserved.
        At sea Thursday 14th September to Tuesday 13th
        September, 1961.
Tuesday 19.9.61
    Due New York
        Mr. & Mrs. J. Wands – No hotel accommodation
        acquired.
        Mr. C. S. Miller – single room with bath reserved
        nights of 19th and 20th September at Commodore
        Hotel.
        At least 6 hours before your departure from New York

170

you must contact the offices of United Airlines at East
Side Terminal, 37th Street and 1st Avenue, Telephone
No. TN. 7-3000 to reconfirm your reservation, time
and reporting place for the following flight.

Thursday 21.9.61	Flight UA. 837
Leave New York	11.30 hrs.
Due Chicago	12.45 hrs.

Two single rooms with bath reserved nights of 21st to
25th September, inclusive, at Palmers House Hotel.
Mr. Wands and Mr. Miller meet Mr. & Mrs. Taylor on
arrival in Chicago and are joined by Mr. Ferguson and
Mr. Brown on 23rd September in Chicago.

MR. & MRS. T. TAYLOR

In accordance with information received from Trans
World Airlines you should report for the following
flight.

Tuesday 26.9.61	Flight TW. 144
Leave Chicago	09.00 hrs
Due New York	11.50 hrs.

MR. W. W. FERGUSON, DIRECTOR.
MR. J. WANDS, MANAGER.
MR. C. S. MILLER, MANAGER.

At least 6 hours before your departure from Chicago
you should contact the offices of United Airlines, 35
E. Monroe, Telephone No. Financial 6-5700 to
reconfirm your reservations, time and reporting place
for the following flight.

Tuesday 26.9.61	Flight UA. 828
Leave Chicago	11.00 hrs.
Due New York	13.55 hrs.

Mr. & Mrs. Taylor – double room with bath reserved
nights of 26th to 28th September, inclusive, at Hotel
Commodore.
Mr. Ferguson – single room with bath reserved nights
of 26th September to 1st October, inclusive, at Hotel

Commodore.

Mr. Wands – single room with bath reserved nights of
26th September to 1st October, inclusive, at Hotel
Commodore.

Mr. Miller – single room with bath reserved nights of
26th to 30th September, inclusive, at Hotel
Commodore.

MR. & MRS. T. TAYLOR

You are in possession of open date flight coupons for
journeys New York/Washington/New York. To effect
your reservations you should contact the offices of
either

> The American Airlines,
> Airlines Building,
> 80 E. 42nd Street,
> New York.
> Telephone No.: Longacre 4-2000

or

> The United Airlines,
> East Side Terminal,
> 37th Street and 1st Avenue,
> New York.
> Telephone No.: WhitePlains T.N. 7-3000

or

> The American Airlines,
> 710 14th Street,
> N.W. Washington.
> Telephone No.: Executive 3-2345

or

> The United Airlines,
> Bender Building,
> Washington.
> Telephone No.: Sterling 3-4700.

At the same time as effecting your reservations you
should have your tickets endorsed and obtain details of
your flights, times and places of reporting.

Under own arrangements with Mr. H. Y. Stewart,

Manager, Tobacco Factory, covering your Washington
and Richmond, Virginia visits.

At least 72 hours before your departure from the
States, you must contact the offices of the B.O.A.C.
either at 535th Avenue, New York 36, Telephone No.:
Murray Hill 7-1600 or at 1124 Connecticut N.W.
Washington, 6. Telephone No.: Executive 3-8508 to
reconfirm your reservation, time and reporting place
for the following flight.

Saturday 14.10.61	Flight BA. 538
Leave New York	21.15 hrs.
Sunday 15.10.61	
Due Glasgow, Prestwick Airport	08.30 hrs.

MR. H. E. Y. STEWART, MANAGER,

Thursday 28.9.61	Flight SK. 913
Leave Glasgow, Prestwick Airport	13.45 hrs.
Due New York	16.05 hrs.

Mr. Stewart under own arrangements in North
American Continent.

Meets up with Directors, Mr. T. Taylor and Mr. W. W.
Ferguson, in Washington, thence to Richmond, and on
completion of business returns to New York for his
departure to the U.K.

At least 72 hours before your departure from the
U.S.A. you must contact the offices of B.O.A.C. at
535th Avenue, New York, 36, Telephone No.: Murray
Hill 7-1600 to reconfirm your reservation, time and
reporting place for the following flight.

Friday 13.10.61	Flight BA. 538
Leave New York	21.15 hrs.
Saturday 14.10.61	
Due Glasgow, Prestwick Airport	08.30 hrs.

MR. W. W. FERGUSON, DIRECTOR.
MR. J. WANDS, MANAGER.

Before your departure from New York you should

contact the offices of The American Airlines, 80
E. 42nd Street or East Side Terminal, 1st Avenue,
Telephone No.: Longacre 4-2000 to reconfirm your
reservation, time and reporting place for the following
flight.

Monday 2.10.61   Flight AA.207
  Leave New York   09.45 hrs.
  Due Washington   11.50 hrs.

Mr. Ferguson – single room with bath reserved nights
of 2nd to 5th October, inclusive, at Statler Hotel.
Mr. Wands – Single room with bath reserved nights of
2nd to 5th October, inclusive, at Statler Hotel.
Mr. Ferguson will be met in Washington by Mr. H. E.
Y. Stewart, Manager, and will then be under
arrangements made by Mr. Stewart until his return to
Washington on 11th October.
Single room with bath reserved for Mr. Ferguson night
of 11th October at the Sheraton Carlton Hotel in
Washington.
Six hours before your departure from Washington, you
should contact The American Airlines at 710 14th
Street, N.W., Telephone No.: Executive 3-2345, to
reconfirm your reservation, time and reporting place
for the following flight.

MR. W. W. FERGUSON, DIRECTOR.

Thursday 12.10.61   Flight AA. 478
  Leave Washington   16.30 hrs.
  Due New York   17.30 hrs.

Single room with bath reserved nights of 12th to 17th
October, inclusive, at Commodore Hotel.
Whilst staying at the Commodore Hotel, officials of the
Cunard Line will hand over embarkation instructions
for the following sea passage.

Wednesday 18.10.61
  At Sea
  Leave New York   'Queen Elizabeth'
                     Single room No. A. 130 with bath reserved.

APPENDIX 1

Monday 23.10.61
    Due Southampton   Late p.m.
    It is expected that you will spend the night of the 23rd
    aboard the Queen Elizabeth due to the late time of
    arrival. You will be met at the docks and taken by
    private car to London to connect with the following
    flight.

Tuesday 24.10.61   Flight BE. 9036
    Leave London, Heathrow Airport   13.30 hrs.
    Due Glasgow, Renfrew Airport   15.05 hrs.

MR. E. B. BROWN, MANAGER.
    Prior to your departure from Chicago you should
    contact the N.W. Airline, 100 South Michigan Avenue,
    Telephone No.: Financial 6-4900 to reconfirm your
    reservation, time and reporting place for the following
    flight.

Tuesday 26.9.61   Flight NW. 211
    Leave Chicago   16.00 hrs.
    Due Winnipeg   20.10 hrs.
    Single room with bath reserved nights of 26th
    September to 1st October, inclusive, at Fort Garry
    Hotel.
    At least 6 hours before your departure from Winnipeg
    you should contact the N.W. Airlines, 404 Main Street,
    Telephone. No.: Spruce 4-4438 to reconfirm your
    reservation, time and reporting place for the following
    flight.

Monday 2.10.61   Flight NW. 224
    Leave Winnipeg   13.35 hrs.
    Due New York   21.00 hrs.
    Single room with bath reserved nights of 2nd and 3rd
    October, inclusive, at Hotel Commodore.
    During your stay in New York, officials of the Cunard
    Line will hand over embarkation notice and luggage
    labels for the following sea passage.

Wednesday 4.10.61
By Sea

Leave New York   'Queen Elizabeth'
Single room M.43 with bath reserved.
Tuesday 10.10.61
Due Southampton
Whilst on board steamer you should purchase your rail
ticket between Southampton and London.

Tuesday 10.10.61	Flight BE. 9154
Leave London, Heathrow Airport	17.50 hrs.
Due Edinburgh, Turnhouse Airport	19.20 hrs.

MR. C. S. MILLER, MANAGER
At least 6 hours prior to your departure from New
York, you should contact T.W. Airlines, East Side
Airline Terminal, 38th Street and 1st Avenue,
Telephone No.: Oxford 5-6000, to reconfirm your
reservation, time and reporting place for the following
flight.

Sunday 1.10.61	Flight TW.237
Leave New York	09.45 hrs.
Due Dayton, Ohio	12.00 hrs.

Single room with bath reserved nights of 1st to 7th
October, inclusive, at Biltmore Hotel.
At least 6 hours before your departure you should
contact The American Airlines in the lobby of your
hotel to reconfirm your reservation, time and reporting
place for the following flight.

Sunday 8.10.61	Flight AA. 582
Leave Dayton, Ohio	10.30 hrs.
Due Cleveland	13.25 hrs.
CHANGE	Flight TC. 276
Leave Cleveland	18.30 hrs.
Due Toronto	19.30 hrs.

Single room with bath reserved nights of 8th and 9th
October, inclusive, at Royal York Hotel.
At least 6 hours before your departure you should
contact the T.C. Airlines in the lobby of your hotel to
reconfirm your reservation, time and reporting place
for the following flight.

176

APPENDIX 1

Tuesday 10.10.61   Flight TC. 376
   Leave Toronto   16.00 hrs.
   Due Montreal   17.20 hrs.
     Single room with bath reserved nights of 10th and
     11th October, at Sheraton Mount Royal Hotel.
     Mr. Miller meets Mr. Wands in Montreal.

MR. J. WANDS, MANAGER
     At least 6 hours prior to your departure from
     Washington you should contact The United Airlines,
     Corner 14th and F. Streets, telephone No.: Sterling 3-
     4700 to reconfirm your reservation, time and place of
     departure for the following flight.

Friday 6.10.61   Flight UA. 263
   Leave Washington   11.40 hrs.
   Due Pittsburg   13.17 hrs.
     Own Hotel arrangements.
     At least 6 hours before your departure from Pittsburg
     you should contact United Airlines at Penn Sheraton
     Hotel, Telephone No.: Locust 3-7555 to reconfirm your
     reservation, time and place of departure for the
     following flight.

Tuesday 10.10.61   Flight UA. 442
   Leave Pittsburg   12.20 hrs.
   Due Buffalo   13.20 hrs.
   CHANGE   Flight AA. 407
   Leave Buffalo   15.05 hrs.
   Due Toronto   15.37 hrs.
     Own Hotel Arrangements.
     At least 6 hours prior to your departure from Toronto,
     you should contact the Trans Canadian Airlines, Bay
     and Temperance Streets, Telephone No.: Walnut 5-
     2311, to reconfirm your reservation, time and place of
     departure for the following flight.

Wednesday 11.10.61   Flight TC. 722
   Leave Toronto   13.40 hrs.
   Due Montreal   14.50 hrs.
     Single room with bath reserved night of 11th October

at Sheraton Mount Royal Hotel.
Mr. Wands meets Mr. Miller in Montreal.
During your stay in Montreal you should contact the
Canadian Pacific Company at Room 115, Windsor
Station, to obtain your embarkation instructions and
luggage labels for the following sea passage.

MR. J. WANDS, MANAGER.
MRS. WANDS,
MR. C. S. MILLER, MANAGER
Thursday 12.10.61
    By Sea
    Leave Montreal   'Empress of Britain'.
            Mr. & Mrs. Wands – double room No. A. 64 reserved.
            Mr. C. S. Miller – single room A. 56 reserved
Wednesday 18.10.61
    Due Greenock

APPENDIX 2

LONDON MALAGA INAUGURAL FLIGHT
8th/14th April, 1962
LIST OF GUESTS

1. Mr. D. Crouch — Marketing Director, Imperial Chemical Industries Ltd., London.
2. Mr. H. Mundy — Coast Lines Ltd.
3. M. C. Eborall — Director, English Electric Co. Ltd., London.
4. Mrs. Eborall
5. Mrs. L. Kennett — Courtaulds Ltd., London.
6. Mr. W. J. Shields — General Motors Ltd., London.
7. Mr. P. Sturman — R. O. Merrell Ltd., London.
8. Mr. D. Burgess — Esso Petroleum Co. Ltd., London.
9. Mr. R. Haynes — Associated Electrical Industries Ltd., London.
10. Mr. A. W. Halifax — J. Lyons & Co. Ltd., London.
11. Miss. C. Depla — International Computers & Tabulators Ltd., London.
12. Mrs. R. Lidyard — Fisons Fertilisers Ltd.
13. Mr. J. Gregory — Transport Manager, Bristol Aeroplane Co.
14. Mr. C. R. Fendy — Manager, Travel Section, Imperial Chemical Industries Ltd., Birmingham.
15. Mr. Noel Wood — Shipping Manager, G.E.C., Coventry.
16. Mr. F. R. W. Webb — U.K. Atomic Energy Authority, Risley.
17. Mr. K. J. Ayrton — Travel Manager, Clayton Analine Co. Ltd., Manchester.

18. Mr. M. Norman Potts   Shipping Manager, Geigy Co., Rhodes, Middleton.

19. Mr. A. MacDougall   Traffic Manager, Scottish Co-operative, Glasgow.

20. Don Andres Vazquez de Prada   Spanish Tourist Office, London.

21. Mr. P. Leuw   Sales Development Manager, B.E.A.

22. Mrs. P. Leuw

23. Mr. B. G. Livesley   Sales Officer (Commercial) London.

INAUGURAL FLIGHT TO MALAGA
14th April, 1962
PROGRAMME.

	HRS	
Apl. 8 Sunday	2000	Check-in Time for guests reporting to West London Air Terminal.,
	2040	Check-in time for guests reporting to London Airport.
	2125 dep.	London Airport by B.E.A. Flight BE. 102 for Malaga.
Apl. 9 Monday	0125 arr.	Malaga, Garcia Morato Airport. Party will be transported to Hotel.
	1930	Cocktails Hotel Triton
	2130	Dinner Hotel El Pinar
Apl. 10 Tuesday	1130	Excursion Costa del Sol
	1230	Drinks Hotel Las Chapas
	1400	Lunch Hotel El Fuerto, Marbella
Apl. 11 Wednesday	1930	Cocktails Sr. Jimenez Lopera, President Chamber of Commerce.
	2130	Gala dinner offered by D.G.T., Gibralfaro (black tie) Club Pimpi, Flamenco dancing.
Apl. 12 Thursday	1500	Excursion to Nerja caves
	2130	Official dinner Ayuntamiento – Malaga Town Hall (black tie)
Apl. 13 Friday	2100	Skal Club dinner

APPENDIX 2

Apl. 14 Saturday   0210   Malaga, Garcia Morato Airport by B.E.A.
                                      Flight BE. 103 for London.
                0615 arr.   London Airport.
                1715 arr.   West London Air Terminal.

LONDON–MALAGA INAUGURAL FLIGHT
8th/14th April, 1962.
HOTEL ACCOMMODATION

1. Mr. D. Crouch	Hotel Carhuela
2. Mr. H. Mundy	–do–
3. Mr. C. Eborall	Hotel Tropicana
4. Mrs. C. Eborall	–do–
5. Mr. P. Leuw (BEA Escort)	–do–
6. Mrs. P. Leuw	–do–
7. Mrs. L. Kennett	–do–
8. Mrs. R. Lidyard	–do–
9. Mr. A. McDougall	–do–
10. Mr. D. Burgess	Hotel Los Nidos
11. Mr. R. Haynes	–do–
12. Mr. F. R. W. Webb	Hotel Playa St. Anna
13. Don Andres Vazquez de Prada	–do–
14. Mr. A. W. Halifax	Hotel Pez Espada
15. Miss C. Depla	–do–
16. Mr. K. J. Ayrton	–do–
17. Mr. M. N. Potts	–do–
18. Mr. B. G. Livesley	
(Sales Officer (Commercial) London)	–do–
19. Mr. C. R. Fenby	Hotel Mir-y-Mar
20. Mr. J. Gregory	–do–
21. Mr. N. Wood	–do–
22. Mr. P. Sturman	Hotel Lloyd
23. Mr. W. J. Shields	–do–

Telegraphic Address: *"Society" Glasgow Telephone NO.: SOUth 2100 Extension*

SCOTTISH CO-OPERATIVE WHOLESALE SOCIETY LTD.
Central Offices:
95 MORRISON STREET, GLASGOW, C.5
All correspondence to be addressed to the Society and not to individuals

Your Ref.

Our Ref. /A/TR/JC   18th April, 1962.

Mr. J. Douglas,
Secretary,

Dear Sir,

B.E.A. Inaugural Flight - London/Malaga.
8th April-14th April 1962

At the invitation of the British European Airways,
Glasgow, and with the approval of the S.C.W.S. Board of
Directors I had the pleasure of participating in the
Inaugural Flight direct from London to Malaga on Sunday
evening, 8th April, 1962. Our party numbered 23 and was
made up of Directors and Managers of the largest
Commercial Houses in the United Kingdom. A list of the
members making up the party is attached.

On my arrival at London Airport I was met by Mr.
B. Livesey, the Commercial Representative of B.E.A., who
introduced me to the rest of the guests. Our flight from
London was most comfortable and was of the duration of
four hours. We arrived in Malaga at 2 a.m. on Monday
morning and after passing through Customs boarded our
transport to make our way to Torremolinos, which is
approximately seven miles from the Airport. Due to the
difficulty in booking the entire party at one Hotel, we
were split up into groups of three and four, spread over
seven Hotels covering a distance of two miles on the
main coastal road. Fortunately, a representative of the
Spanish Tourist Office was with the party acting as
Interpreter and we arrived at our various Hotels with
the correct luggage.

Our programme was well spaced out and consisted
mainly of visiting the different Hotels in the area
where we were met in each instance by the Manager and
escorted around the grounds which, in each case, were
fairly extensive with swimming pool and beautifully laid
out gardens. The Hotels were mostly of Deluxe and Grade

1A Standard and I was impressed by the general layout of
the rooms. Each room had a telephone, hot and cold
washhand basin and shower or bath and, speaking from my
own experience, a most comfortable bed. The catering
arrangements and choice of meals offered was of the
highest standard as was also the service rendered by the
waiters. Prices are fairly reasonable at present with a
general operating minimum of L2 per day per person.
Entertainment was provided in the evenings at Night
Clubs both in Torremolinos and Malaga where we were
again guests of the Spanish Tourist Board. The final
excursion was to the Caves of Nerja followed by a gala
dinner in the evening at which we were the guests of the
Town Council of Malaga, I had the pleasure of meeting
and being introduced to the Deputy Mayor and Chief of
Protocol who were most interested in our reaction as to
what we had seen on our visit. The return flight to
London Airport took place at 3 a.m. on Saturday, 14th
April, and was a very fine flight indeed, touching down
at London Airport at 7 a.m.

I wish to express my appreciation and to thank the
Members of the S.C.W.S. Board for granting me permission
to travel to Spain as the guest of B.E.A. and for the
opportunity of meeting so many outstanding personalities
engaged in this most interesting business of travel.

                    Yours faithfully,
                        Traffic Section.

APPENDIX 3

Miscellanea

J. & A. M^cFARLANE, LIMITED.

HARDWARE AND WOODWARE
MANUFACTURERS AND FACTORS.
IMPORTERS AND EXPORTERS.

DIRECTORS:
DANIEL M^cFARLANE, CHAIRMAN
ROBERT C. M^cFARLANE, MANAGING DIRECTOR.
CHARLES B. M^cFARLANE, O.B.E. WORKS MANAGER.
JAS. M^cFARLANE.

TELEPHONE:
MARYHILL 635.
PRIVATE BRANCH EXCHANGE.
CABLES & TELEGRAMS:
HOUSEHOLD, GLASGOW.

ALBERT WORKS
SPRINGBANK STREET
GLASGOW, N.W.

11th August, 1942.

Dear Mrs. Macdougall,

It is with deep regret that we learn that your son has died of wounds in the Far East.

We were always hoping that he had managed to escape safely from the overrun territory and the news of his death has come as a great shock to us all.

Andrew was very popular with everyone here and the management had a very high opinion of him. He was always so willing and obliging and so keen about his duties.

The directors and members of the staff tender their deepest sympathy with you in your sad bereavement. May the thought that your son has laid down his life for his friends be a source of pride and comfort to you in your great sorrow.

Yours sincerely,

R.C.McFarlane

J. & A. M^cFARLANE, LIMITED.

HARDWARE AND WOODWARE
MANUFACTURERS AND FACTORS.
IMPORTERS AND EXPORTERS.

DIRECTORS:
DANIEL M^cFARLANE, CHAIRMAN.
ROBERT C. M^cFARLANE, MANAGING DIRECTOR.
CHARLES S. M^cFARLANE, O.B.E. WORKS MANAGER.
JAS. M^cFARLANE.

TELEPHONE:
MARYHILL 635.
PRIVATE BRANCH EXCHANGE.
CABLES & TELEGRAMS:
"HOUSEHOLD, GLASGOW.

ALBERT WORKS
SPRINGBANK STREET
GLASGOW, N.W.

To whom it may concern:-

5th July, 1946

    This is to certify that Andrew G. Macdougall entered our employment as a lad in November 1932. After experience in our warehouse he latterly had charge of the Holloware Dept.

    We found him to be honest and reliable in every way and he carried out his duties to our entire satisfaction.

    He joined the R.A.F. in March 1940 and was a prisoner of War in Japanese hands for 3 1/2 years. We would be very glad to have him back with us, but on medical advice he has been recommended to try to get an outdoor job.

    We feel sure he will give every satisfaction to any one in need of his services.

Yours faithfully,
J. & A. MCFARLANE LIMITED.

R.C.McFarlane

THE GUTHRIE SAGA

MEDICAL HISTORY OF A G MACDOUGALL
Born 11th October 1918

Age	Description
2 months	Whooping Cough
5 years	Scarlet Fever
16 years	Broken Collar-Bone (twice)
21 years	RAF medical passed A1 vision 20/20
23 years	Singapore evacuated but captured in Padang, Sumatra
24 years	JAP POW October, 1942 commenced building of Burma Railway

Dress: G-string only in jungle, no medicine available. Suffered malarial stages BTST and CT (hallucinating stage) three finger spleen. This latter stage was combined with dysentery and beriberi and reduced weight to six stone. On release on August 17th 1945 we were flown to Rangoon where I was treated for hookworm.

On return to England I was medically examined in London by an RAF doctor and classified as C3 the lowest category, he also advised me my X-ray had shown that I had been attacked by tuberculosis but that my immune system had sealed it off. There was talk of a pension entitlement before he went to see the senior medical officer but no further mention was made on his return. My last attack of cerebral malaria was in Scotland in 1957. I emigrated to South Australia in 1963.

During 1980 in one operation I had my hernia repaired and two large kidney stones removed. Later, in 1981 my prostate was removed.

During 1990 I claimed a pension from the British Government and was examined by a physician and by a psychiatrist. I was 1% off being awarded a pension for hypertension with associated features and instead was given a grant of approx £5,000 with further examinations every 4 years, first due 1994. I was warned a good number of years ago to be on the lookout for any rash which may appear on my body which, if it did not clear up, to have checked out. I was also advised not to accept cortisone for any purpose due to the possibility that I may still have a tropical parasite in my system (*Strongyloides stercoralis*).

During 1996 I made a further claim to the Blackpool Pension Department in the UK. A medical examination was arranged through the Australian Veteran Affairs Department and I was examined by Dr Edmonds in Hervey Bay, the report being forwarded to Blackpool. Their

186

decision was that I was 40% disabled due to the effects of malaria, beriberi, and dysentery. I was granted a pension of approximately £50 sterling per week from early 1996 with the proviso for a further medical examination in the year 2000.

The Opalised Plesiosaur

White Cliffs N.S.W.

THIS RARE 8½ ft. LONG OPALISED SKELETON OF A PLESIOSAUR IS THE MOST COMPLETE YET FOUND. IT IS ESTIMATED TO HAVE LIVED OVER 100,000,000 YEARS AGO IN THE DINOSAUR ERA.

NOW

ON DISPLAY

White Cliffs

TOWN FACILITIES INCLUDE...

☆ General store, accommodation 4 rooms—Phone 11

☆ Hotel, accommodation 5 rooms—Phone 6

☆ Post Office

☆ Caravan Park—Phone 18

☆ Hospital (Sister, and R.F.D.S.)

☆ School Primary—Phone 17

☆ Aerodrome, D.C.A. Licence

☆ Church services

☆ Large new public hall

☆ Water available

☆ Regularly serviced by road freight carrier and "Silver City Air Taxis"

Wilcannia accommodation

☆ 3 Hotels and the Wilcannia Motel

WHITE CLIFFS IS AUSTRALIA'S OLDEST, LARGE OPAL FIELD . . . ITS 50 REGISTERED DUGOUTS MAKE IT EASTERN AUSTRALIA'S BIGGEST UNDERGROUND SETTLEMENT.

Discovered back in 1887 by a party of kangaroo shooters, it was rapidly brought to prominence by the miners and buyers like Woolaston & Murphy who established an overseas market for the rare gem, which eclipsed in beauty the existing Hungarian opal.

More than 50,000 opal dumps offer the tourist a chance to find cuttable material. Outside the field there is a vast potential for prospecting.

Suggested Itinerary

☆ Inspect the Plesiosaur
☆ Tour of Field
☆ Visit a Walk-in-Mine
☆ Advertised underground homes to visit
☆ View Opal Displays, Pictures, Pottery and Leather Work
☆ See an Opal Cutter at work

The skeleton was found on the 3 metre level in a shaft being sunk for opal on Sullivan's Hill, White Cliffs. Once the miner, Ken Harris, realized the significance of those odd looking pieces of opal sticking out of the side of the shaft, great care was taken to expose the rest of the skeleton. Once exposed, he decided to give the Australian Museum the chance of examining it, so they were contacted. To avoid possible theft of parts of the skeleton, the discovery was kept a careful secret until Dr. Ritchie and Bob Jones of the Sydney Museum had time to encase it in plaster and take it back.

It was while it was in the museum in Sydney that the museum authorities expressed a great interest in buying the fossil. The figure offered, however, was much below the miner's aims, so it was decided it would be taken back to the place of origin where it would act as a major attraction for tourism.

THE CAMP COMMANDER
AND
HIS ASSISTANTS

Major H. Waters, M.B.E.   ...   *Commander, R.A.P.W.I. Camp*
14 Punjab Regt.   *" Belvedere "*

Capt. D. C. Charlier, M.C.   ...   *Officer i/c British Wing*
Kings Own Scottish Borderers

Major D. Webb   ...   *Officer i/c Indian Wing.*
7 Gurkha Rifles

Capt. J. Lyle, A.C.C   ...   *Catering Adviser*

Capt. D. A. Read   ...   *Recreation & Entertainments*
8 Gurkha Rifles   *Officer*

Miss J. Christensen   ...   *Lady Superviser.*

LADY ASSISTANTS   ...   *From Bengal Womens Voluntary*
                         Service.

Prepared by Public Relations Branch Eastern Command for H.Q. Transit Group,
303 L. of C. Area.   *Printed by " Essco Press," Calcutta.*

« BELVEDERE »

ARMY COMMANDER'S MESSAGE

TO ALL SERVICEMEN AND CIVILIANS ARRIVING IN BENGAL
FROM FAR EASTERN COUNTRIES HITHERTO OCCUPIED BY
THE JAPANESE I SEND MY WARMEST WELCOME. I HOPE
YOUR STAY IN CALCUTTA WILL BE COMFORTABLE AND
THAT THE REUNION WITH YOUR FAMILIES AT HOME WILL
NOT BE LONG DELAYED.

R n o'connor

General,
General Officer Commanding-in-Chief, Eastern Command.

7TH SEPTEMBER, 1945.

"BELVEDERE" HISTORY

"**B**ELVEDERE" where you are now being accommodated was used as the official residence of Lieutenant-Governors of Bengal from 1854 up to the time of transfer of the Imperial Capital to Delhi, since when it was retained as the official residence of His Excellency the Viceroy during his visits to Calcutta.

Although "Belvedere" was not purchased as the official residence of the Lieutenant-Governor of Bengal till 1854, it had been the private house of Governors before the time of Warren Hastings who purchased it for £7,500 somewhere about the year 1774 and sold it to a Colonel Tolly, the excavator of Tolly's Nullah, in 1780.

Its early history is somewhat mysterious and there is nothing on record to show exactly who started building it or when or for what purpose. One writer asserts that it was commenced by Price Azim-us-Sham in 1700. Certain it is that it stood at that time in the lonely tiger infested jungles of a low lying marshy village which was later to be known as Alipore.

It was during Colonel Tolly's occupation of "Belvedere" that Hastings fought his memorable duel with a Mr. Francis (a member of council) at half past five on the morning of the 17th August 1780. The stage for this dramatic settling of a question of honour which affected Hastings was set in the fields of Alipore. Close by "Belvedere". Mr. Francis' shot whistled past the Governor General's ear but Hastings wounded his opponent who was carried into "Belvedere" and attended to by the Surgeon General of Fort William.

From then until 1854 "Belvedere" passed through several hands until it became the official residence of the Lieutenant-Governor and later still, once more the official residence of a Governor General. Shortly after 1825 it came into the occupatio of the Prinsep Family who finally bought it outright in 184 and sold it to the East India Company in 1854 for Rs. 80,000. By this time the orignal extensive grounds had diminished considerably.

Since then the house has been improved from time to time by successive occupants. Its architecture is of a pre-Italian Renaissance style developed on an ordinary Anglo-Indian building. The construction of the verandah on the East side and the reconstruction of a more commodious West wing were carried out in 1868—1870 and between 1877 and 1879 the whole of the main centre facade was added and also a wooden floor placed on the central ballroom.

With the advent of World War II most of the charm of "Belvedere" has disappeared under its sombre purplish camouflage and the very necessary improvisations carried out to make the building suitable for an important RAF Headquarters.

FOR YOUR CONVENIENCE

To enable you to obtain as much assistance as possible and to make your stay as comfortable as it can be a number of amenities have been arranged for you at " Belvedere ".

In the Gallery of the upstairs Ballroom there is a W.V.S. Canteen and a library.

In the Ballroom you will find: —

> THE PAYMASTER.
>
> SOLDIERS' SAILORS' & AIRMENS' FAMILIES ASSOCIATION.
>
> INCORPORATED SOLDIERS' SAILORS' AND AIRMENS' HELP SOCIETY.
>
> RED CROSS INFORMATION BUREAU.
>
> CURRENT AFFAIRS & RESETTLEMENT BUREAU.
>
> POST OFFICE.
>
> A CANTEEN.
>
> A SHOP.
>
> A BAR.

In other parts of the grounds you will find: —

> A TAILOR.
>
> A BARBER.
>
> A SWIMMING POOL.

Separate announcements will tell you about: —

> E. N. S. A. PERFORMANCES.
>
> CINEMA SHOWS.